Mudras of the Buddha (His Life and Works)

Also by Dhiravamsa

ALSO BY WISDOM MOON PUBLISHING
Nirvana Upside Down (2012)
Healing through Pure Minfulness (2014)

BY OTHER PUBLISHERS
(ARRANGED IN CHRONOLOGICAL ORDER
OF THE BOOK'S FIRST EDITION IN THE GIVEN LANGUAGE)

Insight Meditation (UK: 1966, 1967)
Beneficial Factors for Meditation (UK: 1967)
The Real Way to Awakening (UK: 1968)
A New Approach to Buddhism (UK: 1971)
"Theravāda Meditation" in *Secrets of the Lotus,* edited by Donald K. Swearer (USA: 1972)
The Middle Path of Life (UK: 1974, 1980; USA: 1988)
The Way of Non-Attachment (UK: 1975, 1984)
Angenommen Sie fühlen sich elend (Austria: 1979)
Das meditative Leben. Ein neuer Weg zum Buddhismus (Germany: 1980)
La via del non attaccamento (Italy: 1980)
The Dynamic Way of Meditation (UK: 1982, 1989)
La voie du non-attachement (France: 1982, 2010)
La meditación dinámica (Argentina: 1983)
L'attention: Source de plénitude (France: 1983, 2010)
La via dinamica della meditazione (Italy: 1983)
Turning to the Source (USA: 1990)
De ongedwongen weg (Netherlands: 1990)
La vía del no apego (Spain: 1991, 1993, 1994, 1998, 2010)
Meditación y eneagrama (Spain: 1992, 1998, 2000, 2007)
Retorno al origen (Spain: 1992)

La vía del despertar (Spain: 1996)

Cómo liberarnos del sufrimiento (Spain: 1998)

Palabras de sabiduría del Buda:
Análisis psicoespiritual del comentario del Dhammapada (Spain: 2000)

La leyenda de Shriton y Manorah: Las pruebas del amor consciente
(Spain: 2001)

Una nueva visión del Budismo (Spain: 2005)

El gran río de la consciencia (Spain: 2005)

The Power of Conscious Love:
A Psycho-Spiritual Analysis of a Classic Thai Tale of Shrithon-Manorah
(USA: 2006)

Der Weg zum Nicht-Anhaften (Germany: 2006)

Crisis y solución: Unión de opuestos (Spain: 2008)

Meditación vipassana y gestalt (Spain: 2008)

Un atajo a la iluminación:
Guía para la práctica de la atención plena (Spain, 2009, 2013)

Shedding Light on Each Eneatype's Mind:
Enneagram System of Personality/Character (Spain: 2009)

Vipassana and Gestalt Therapy (Thailand: 2009)

Iluminando la mente de cada eneatipo: Edición bilingüe español-inglés
(Spain: 2009)

Ο Δρόμος της μη προσκόλλησης:
Η Άσκηση του Ενορατικού Διαλογισμού - Α' Μέρος (Greece: 2007)

Εννεάγραμμα και Αυτομεταμόρφωση:
Με Ενορατικό Διαλογισμό Βιπασσάνα - Τα Εννέα Πρόσωπα της Ψυχής
(Greece: 2008)

Медитация, которая Действительно работает, Випассана (Russia: 2010)

Unión De Los Opuestos (Spain, 2012)

La vía dinámica de la meditación (Spain, 2012)

La via del risveglio:
Instruzioni per la meditazione vipassana (Italy, 2013)

Volviendo a la Naturaleza Primordial (Spain, 2014)

Sankthong, a Thai classic Tale with original Psycho-spiritual Analysis (Spain, 2015; in Spanish and English editions)

Mindfulness & Financial Investment
co-authored with José Diego Alarcón (Spain, 2016; in Spanish and English editions)

Mudras of the Buddha (His Life and Works)

Each Illustrated by its Story and Event that Took Place in the Buddha's Time

Dhiravamsa

Wisdom Moon Publishing
2016

MUDRAS OF THE BUDDHA (HIS LIFE AND WORKS)
EACH ILLUSTRATED BY ITS STORY AND EVENT THAT TOOK PLACE IN THE BUDDHA'S TIME

Copyright © 2016 Wisdom Moon Publishing, LLC

All rights reserved. Tous droits réservés.

No part of this work may be copied, reproduced, recorded, stored, or translated, in any form, or transmitted by any means electronic, mechanical, or other, whether by photocopy, fax, email, internet group postings, or otherwise, without written permission from the copyright holder, *except for brief quotations* in reviews for a magazine, journal, newspaper, broadcast, podcast, etc., or in scholarly or academic papers, *when quoted with a full citation to this work.*

Published by Wisdom Moon Publishing LLC
San Diego, CA, USA

Wisdom Moon™, the Wisdom Moon logo™, *Wisdom Moon Publishing*™, and *WMP*™ are trademarks of Wisdom Moon Publishing LLC.

www.WisdomMoonPublishing.com

ISBN 978-1-938459-64-1 (softcover, alk. paper)
ISBN 978-1-938459-66-5 (eBook)
LCCN 2016952567

Front cover: digitally adapted image of a Reclining Buddha, Hua Hin, Thailand.

Mudras of the Buddha (His Life and Works)

Acknowledgment

The author is deeply indebted to the Most Venerable Phra Vimala Dharma (Chob Anucârî Mahathera), the original author of the Thai Book: *Phra Buddharoop Pang Tang Tang*, which was published in 2533/1990 for commemorating his 89th Birthday.

I, the present author, knew him personally and admired him with a profound gratitude and an indescribable appreciation. Without his book, this present work would have been impossible to be published in English and made available to the Western Hemisphere.

Dedication

This work is dedicated to my parents, Nai Nuan and Nang Indra, for their unbounded love and their wonderful ways of bringing me up as well as their benevolent support.

Mudras of the Buddha (His Life and Works)

Mudra 1

Mudra 1

Mudra of Taking up Monkhood

In this mudra the Buddha was seated in the samadhi posture with his left hand placed on his lap while the right hand is raised up to the chest level bending its palm toward the left, which indicates the stabilization of mind for renouncing the world and taking up the monkhood. In this posture there is no radiant light shining through his head because such light would appear only when his full enlightenment is achieved. Another name for this posture is that of **renouncing** the world.

Illustrating Story:

When the Buddha-to-be, in another word, **bodhisatta** (Sanskrit, **bodhisattva**), was born a *deva of delight* (dusita deva) and lived in that delightful heaven (dusita), those great brahmas and devas of all the heavenly worlds approached him (dusita deva). Then they requested that he gave up his heaven and be born in the human world in order to become a fully enlightened Buddha so that he could teach Dharma together with its practices for helping all sentient beings liberate themselves from pain and suffering as well as from the cycle of birth-death-life (samsara).

Then and there the bodhisattva (dusita deva) was considering circumstances and situations of both heavenly and human worlds and came to a realization of five categories required for his descending and entering human form. They are: time, place, family, mother, and age. After realizing fully that all those five categories were utterly appropriate he then accepted their humble request. So, he abandoned the dusita heaven and descended in the womb of Siri Maha Maya, Queen of King Suddhodana who was then the ruler of a small kingdom of Sakyans with Kapilavatthu as its capital city.

Now we arrive at a question of who the Buddha is

The personal name of the Buddha is *Siddhartha*. He is the only son of King Suddhodana and Queen Siri Maha Maya who reigns over the Kingdom of Sakyans (at present it is located near the border between Nepal and India.) At the age of sixteen he gets married to Princess Yasodharâ, and thirteen years later they have a son named "Râhula." When he reaches twenty-nine years of age, he renounces his kingdom and becomes a monk. Six years after that he achieves full enlightenment under the Bodhi Tree at Buddhagaya. Finally, he passes away under the pair of Sala Trees in Kusinara at the age of eighty.

About his birth

Prince Siddhartha was born under the Banyan tree when his mother was on her way to give birth at her parents' home in the Kingdom of Koliyans located on the other side of the River Rohini. Because she could not reach her parents' kingdom due to the fact that her child was so ready to be born, she decided to go to the Garden of Lumbini (Lumminde at present) and gave birth there. As soon as he was born, he walked seven steps and exclaimed: *Aggohamasmi lokasmim jettho settho anuttaro ayantima me jati natthidani punabbhavo*, which means, *"In this world I am the Chief, the Most Self-Developed One, and the Excellent One. This birth is the final one; and no longer exists any new existence."* At that moment, the earth trembled with a great uproar as if it were expressing its joy and delight for the coming into the world of the Buddha-to-be. This is the first perplexity regarding the prince whose fate would take him to the Buddhahood.

Let us explore the meaning of the perplexity. Number seven indicates the completion of action and/or fate as shown in the Buddha's life. That is to say, after becoming the Buddha through his own effort and intelligence he traveled, taught the

Dharma, and established his Doctrine and Discipline (dharma-vinaya) in seven states in the ancient India, technically known as "Jambúdípa." The act of walking symbolically refers to the movement and activity of life inwardly directed by the natural, free flow of the life stream, or the *slender threads*, to use Robert A. Johnson's terminology.[1] As a matter of fact, Siddhartha did just that — followed these slender threads — all his life from his youth up till he reached the full enlightenment. Thereafter, he (as the Buddha, the enlightened one) followed his all-seeing eye of enlightened wisdom showing him clearly and precisely what to do and where to move.

This matter of exclaiming right after being born into life signifies the capacity to share with all fellow beings the truth, immediate wisdom, and illimitable or unconditional love through his great compassion. It is true that throughout his life the Buddha worked really hard in selflessly helping his monks, nuns, and people realize the truth and accomplish the immeasurable freedom, or at least find the right path to such goals. He literally slept only two hours a night (plus two hours of deep meditation soon after getting up, that is from four to six in the morning.) The rest of the time was devoted to teaching and working with his Order of Monks, his Order of Nuns, his lay supporters, and those interested in meeting or discussing with him and/or needing his help regarding spiritual matters and clarifications of the truth (dharma) which was rather confusing in those days.

If we do not take things literally but pay keen attention to the symbols (including words) employed, or expressed, we will certainly find the meaning. In addition, we will be able to relate to them meaningfully as well as to benefit greatly, having such meaningfulness in our lives and in our everyday living. For this

---

[1] For more, see Chap. 6: REALIZING THE PATH OF TRANSFORMATION in *A New Vision of Buddhism* by the same author.

reason, we don't disregard the seemingly irrational and unscientific matters as useless pieces of imagination or superstition. We can learn so much from symbols, dreams, fantasies, images, and imaginations if we pay vital attention to them, since they represent, and pour out of, the *unconscious* in our deep psyche and in the depths of our being. All words are symbolic since they are the most popular means that the unconscious and ancient, profound wisdom utilize to communicate thereby with us.

Now, concerning the actual birth of the Buddha: he was born in the Beautiful Garden of Lumbini surrounded by fresh greens and lively nature in the month of May, which marks the beginning of the rainy season in India. This implies that the birth of New Consciousness requires naturalness, simplicity, and purity of the heart. It is also said in the Greek myth in which Cadmus with his three brothers and his mother set out searching for his beautiful sister, Europa, who was taken away by the bull (symbolic Zeus). After a long, long journey they arrived at an extraordinarily beautiful place with green fields, lively forests, and mighty mountains surrounding it. There the youngest brother told his party that he did not want to go on searching for his sister any longer because the journey has been too long since they left home and they had looked for her without any sign of success in finding her. He further said that she might have died already, or if she would still be alive, they wouldn't recognize her. Therefore, he decided to build his Kingdom and settle there. And so he did with the assistance of all his brothers, his mother, and some new travelers who joined them on the journey. This also indicates the birth of New Consciousness symbolized by the construction of a New Kingdom in such a beautiful nature.

It has been clear that the myth concerning the Buddha's birth informs us not only of the coming into the world of the Great Being, but of where and how the New Consciousness could arise in each of us individually. Certainly, *solitude,* not just as an excluded place in a lovely, pure nature, but the *inner solitude* in which the mind becomes quiet, still, and well stabilized, is the golden key for opening the doors to the discovery of treasures within and thereby the *Golden World* will be found. Let us, then, take solitude not in the negative sense of isolation or an escape from life, but in its true sense of being solitary but one with all, meaning, a total connectedness and all-embracingness without any psychological confusion. With this type of solitude one will certainly be able to accommodate New Consciousness, nurturing it with keen caring, and attentively watching it grow.

His Attainment to Enlightenment

After giving up the opportunity for becoming a great emperor, he left the royal palace, his wife, his newly born child, and his parents, at night; and then took on being a form of monk at dawn. After that he searched for the right teacher and discovered the two distinguished spiritual masters: They were Âlara Kalama and Udaka Ramaputta. He industriously studied and practiced all their teachings and methods of practice for achieving enlightenment and freedom until those great masters in history recognized him as equal to themselves. Realizing that what he was actually looking for had not been accomplished, he took leave of them and continued seeking after the truth by himself. At this point in time, he experimented with the practice of fasting and he did it to his utmost until he almost died. As the story said, during that period of severe fasting, one day he could not move his body and therefore, lay down completely still under a tree and went through a near-death experience. Fortunately, a young boy who took care of cattle discovered him and out of his compassion for the Monk Gotama (the Buddha's name known at the time of his monkhood), he decided to help him. The young cowherd went to milk his cow and brought a full bottle to pour into the monk's mouth. (The Monk Gotama must have been semi-unconscious, for he knew nothing until he came back to his senses and opened his eyes.) After swallowing the milk and assimilating it fully he looked around and saw a young boy standing at a near distance. He then asked who the boy was and what he did to bring him back from his exhausted fasting. When he was informed of the fact that the boy gave him the bottle of milk by pouring it in his mouth, he then realized what was happening. He thanked the boy for his good deed and great help; whilst the boy apologized for touching the holy man like him since he was born from the untouchable family (the untouchable people have no rights to touch the holy people). The Monk Gotama simply told him that there was nothing to apologize for because he did nothing wrong, and then he went on saying, "One is not noble or ignoble because of his birth from a noble family or from a poor family. But the good deeds or bad ones make people good or evil."

That late afternoon, the Monk Gotama happened to hear a song sung by the country girls in a forest nearby as they were collecting firewood. The content of the song was that in playing a violin if the strings are too loose, they would not produce a good music; on the contrary, if they are too tight, they might break. But good music can be produced from a violin whose strings are just right, that is, neither too tight nor too loose. Through grasping the meaning of the song, the Monk Gotama woke up from his lack of awareness or ignorance and realized that his practice of fasting was too severe and was absolutely to no avail. So he gave it up right there, and returned to his normal eating. He thanked the girls with all his heart for helping him receive such invaluable vision, at a distance, of course!

From then on, he followed the middle way, cultivating Right or Impeccable Mindfulness and Visionary Insights up to the point where his mind was clear and his body relaxed and clean. In the Eve of the Full Moon Day of May, after having made a strong determination that he would not get up from his meditation seat until the *Full Enlightenment* was accomplished, although his bones might be broken into pieces, his blood would dry up, and his flesh might get rotten, he sat there under the Bodhi Tree (the Tree of Perfect Knowledge) in front of the River Neranjará, facing the East. As he was sinking deeply into the meditative state, he encountered two overwhelming passions: *attachment and fear* manifested to him in form of seductive young women and a scene of a battlefield.

The first images that appeared to him were the pictures of the three beautiful, young women whose names are *tanhá (craving or thirst), rága (passionate desire), and arati (aversion)*. They manipulated him and seduced him by showing various parts of their bodies together with saying to him that enjoying the pleasures of senses in life is much better than sitting still and doing nothing but hoping for the best. They asked him to give up such useless practices and return to the ordinary life in the world. At first he was slightly tempted by their performance, but later realized that it was the manifestation of his *delusive consciousness* in which are contained the inseparable passions of attachment, craving, and fear. So he let them be, and continued deepening his meditation. This time he saw himself in great danger since the images of warships, bombing aircraft, and armed forces appear in such way that they are all pointing their destructive weapons toward him. At this point in time he became so frightened that one of his hands suddenly slipped out of the meditation posture and his eyes open up slightly. Realizing that it is simply the mental picture symbolizing his fear, particularly the fear of death, he then returned to his meditation and continued his profound inner journey until the dawn of the day. At the moment of the rising of the sun and the disappearing of darkness, he reached complete awakening, full enlightenment and therefore became *Buddha (Fully Awakened One)*.

The Buddha's enlightenment consists of three principal factors. The first factor is the vivid memory of his detailed past lives, which explode to him at the first watch of the night (around 10 p.m.). The second factor involves the visionary insights into birth, death, and rebirth of all beings in the universe, arising in him at the second watch of the night (around 2 a.m.). The third factor is *Inner Knowledge and Insightful Wisdom* concerning all the defilements and contaminations within his consciousness that have been fully purified and totally transformed with no destructive elements left unfinished, arising in him at the last watch of the night (around 6 a.m.).

In actual fact, the moment he became fully awakened to the Noble Truths and from the psychological and spiritual forms of sleep or reached enlightenment five significant things rose in him, they are, Awakened Eye of Seeing things as they are (cakkhu), Insight or Profound Inner Vision (ñâna), All-Knowing Wisdom (paññâ), Illimitable and Illuminating Knowledge (vijjâ), and Unbounded Light (âloka). Together with those five factors he experientially realized the Four Noble Truths, namely, Suffering, Arising of Suffering, Cessation of Suffering, and the Middle Path[2] that leads to the Cessation of Suffering, which is the Realization of Nirvana. Finally, he exclaimed that his immeasurable Freedom, Full Awakening, and Realization of Nirvana are irreversible, the Holy (Whole) Life has been fully lived, all needs to be done has been done, and there is no more to do (the life's journey is completed).

---

[2] The Buddha's Middle Path consists of Eight Factors, namely, Perfect Wisdom or Right Understanding, and Right Thinking (wisdom group); Right Action, Right Speech, and Right Livelihood (ethics group); Invincible Perseverance, Impeccable Mindfulness, and Right Focused Concentration or Firmly Stabilized Mind technically known as Samadhi (meditation group).

Mudra 2

Mudra 2

Mudra of Reflection

The Buddha image of this mudra is seated in the samadhi posture with his left hand holding that bowl which is laid on his lap, while his right hand is raised to the chest level with his eyes cast down. This is the gesture or mudra of reflection.

Illustrating Story:

After Siddhartha has taken on a form of monk or recluse (from now on we will call him "Monk Gotama"), he told Channa, his faithful personal attendant, to carry back to the Royal Palace his garments and to inform his parents, wife, and all members of his royal families of this radical change taken up by him. He further instructed Channa to let them all know that he would return home for a visit with them after Full Enlightenment has been reached and Nirvana Experientially Realized.

Naturally Channa became extremely sad because of the painful deprivation from his unbounded love and reverential respect for him. Also, the similar, unbearable sorrow occurred to the horse named "Kanthaka", an indispensable vehicle of Siddhartha. It was so unbearably painful that the faithful Kanthaka fell dead a short while after parting from Monk Gotama, its utmost lovable and reverently respectful master.

Upon his arrival back to the city Channa reported to King Suddhodana, Queen Maha Maya, Princess Bimba (Siddhartha's wife), and all the royal relatives all the incidents that happened to the Prince. Needless to say how painful sadness and excruciating sorrow was that they felt; nonetheless they would patiently wait for his return as he promised with Channa.

Let us get back to Monk Gotama. For a period of seven days after becoming a monk he did not eat anything apart from enjoying his monkhood in a forest with its name of *anupiya-ambavana (lovely mango grove)*, but entering the eighth day he took his alms-bowl and went in Rajagaha City for collecting food following a tradition of recluses, the way by which monks earn their living. He was walking mindfully with all his faculties in control but relaxed and radiant. He then received plenty of food given freely and with respect by the donors lining up a long side of the city street.

When he had enough food for the day he left the city through the same gate where he entered. Not too far from Rajagaha, the Capital City of Magadha State, there was a long range of beautiful mountains. Monk Gotama found an agreeable mountain called **Manthava** with a very pleasant and lovely slope where he could sit down and have his meal from his alms-bowl. Looking at the food and examining it thoroughly he thought that it was neither so neat nor was it so beautiful as he used to eat at his palace, so he got a disgusting feeling and declined to put any of it in his mouth.

Up to this point, he reflected with mindfulness on his situations both old and new, and realized completely that he was no longer a Prince but a monk who lives on what's given without making choices, but with a mental attitude of equanimity, gratitude, and acceptance. With such unsurpassed realization through his heedful reflection, he then ate his first meal gracefully and with impeccable awareness.

ᓂ
Mudra 3

Mudra 3

Mudra of Self-mortification

In this mudra the Buddha was seated in the samadhi posture with both hands laid on top of each other; that is to say, the right hand is placed on top of the left hand. His robe is covering each half of his arms while from the right arm it falls down to rest on his lap (in some other places the robe falls down from both arms and stays in good order on his lap). Obviously, his entire physical body becomes so extremely thin that the bones and nerves stand out visibly.

Illustrating Story:

Since the first day of his entry in Rajagaha City and many citizen saw him as a special monk whose sense faculties were so composed and outstanding that each movement of his mindful walk along the street became utterly precise and strikingly calm, so one of the king's man happened to be present at the scene witnessed everything that particular morning. He then reported to his king his eyewitness of such an unusual monk. King Bimbisara, the Great King of Magadha State (a very large and powerful State) became quite excited about Monk Gotama and therefore, wanted to meet with him. One good day he together with his spiritual advisor and significant ministers left for his residence in the Manthava Mountain outside of his Capital City in order to meet and converse with him.

At first the King inquired into his name, birthplace, family, and country where he was born and grew up. Upon learning that he was a former prince of the Sakyans and his father was a king and reigned over the Sakyan Kingdom, he thought that perhaps Monk Gotama was a victim of a severe conflict in his kingdom. Therefore, King Bimbisara offered him one half of his super-power Magadha so that he could enjoy ruling it side by side with him. To this generous offer Monk Gotama humbly declined to accept it informing him of his sole purpose of seeking full enlightenment in order to liberate all sentient beings from pain, suffering, and the birth-life[3]-death cycle so that all those beings could be blessed with immeasurable freedom and everlasting, supreme peace of nirvana.

Soon after that he searched for the right teacher and discovered two distinguished masters. He diligently studied and practiced their teachings and methods of practice until he accomplished all of them. Then he realized experientially that those achievements were not the ultimate goal that he was seeking, let alone the right way to enlightenment and realization of nirvana. So, he left them one after the other, and continued searching for the right path.

Then, he encountered practices broadly believed to be the ways to enlightenment. They were called **self-mortification**, which consists of three phases, namely, (1) ***pressing tightly all the teeth against one another, and pressing hard the tongue against the palate up to the point that the sweat was pouring out of his armpits.*** As a result, he suffered tremendous pain and agony. Nonetheless, he was resolutely determined to live through such hard, painful feeling in order to bring the practice to completion. Once he came to a realization that it was not the way, he gave it up, and then tried another practice. This time, (2) he was practicing a **breath manipulation** by controlling and holding tightly the inhaling breath for a long period of time after each inhalation before letting out of the air with an exhalation. When the air could not go out either through the nose or the mouth, the ears got seemingly blocked and a heavy noise ***"ooh, ooh"*** was produced and therefore, he got a severe headache together with an awful stomachache. Once again, he gave up such useless, self-mortifying practice; and yet continued trying

---

[3] A heavily conditioned life.

the third phase of self-mortification. This time, (3) it was a practice of an extreme **fasting**[4]. He began with reducing the quantity of food, meaning, eating less and less until eventually not eating at all. In so doing, his body became withered, dry, dull, and with little light and lack of vitality. He was so skinny that the entire physical form almost turned into a skeleton. Fortunately, a young cowherd as previously cited saved him. He then gave up such an unprofitable, useless, and highly dangerous self-mortification altogether.

After having put into test and sincere experimentation Monk Gotama turned to his own resources and found the **middle way**[5], the path between two extreme practices, namely, **self-mortification** (extreme spiritualism) and **self-indulgence** (extreme materialism). He then followed the middle path with diligence and intelligence, and finally achieved full enlightenment on the full moon day of May. It was a complete six-year-search.

---

[4] See details of that practice on the section on His Attainment to Enlightenment, under Mudra 1.
[5] Details of the middle path are found in footnote no. 2.

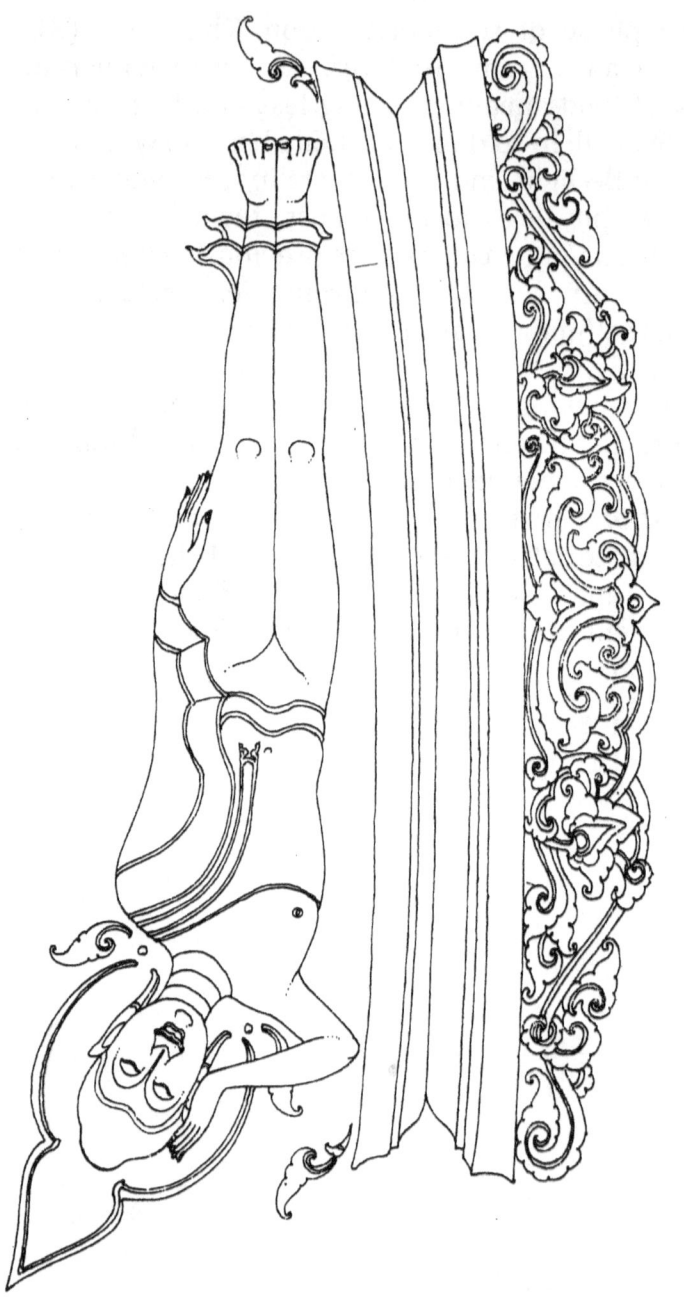

Mudra 4

Mudra 4

Dreaming Mudra

In this mudra the Buddha is found resting in the lying posture in which he lays his body on the right side (a position of a sleeping lion – sihaseyyasa). His left hand is placed along side the body while his right hand is laid on the floor with the palm raised up for supporting the chin and with eyes gently closed. (The Buddha always sleeps in this manner.)

Illustrating Story:

After he had utterly given up the self-mortification practice, Monk Gotama devoted himself enthusiastically to the mental training, cultivating and making much of mindfulness, as well as developing insights. This new development he discovered through his own insightful capacity since it did not exist, nor was it ever practiced before.

Let us go back for a little while to the period when he was severely practicing self-mortification. During that time there were five ascetics who believed convincingly in such a practice as the way to enlightenment, who went out to search for an enlightened master. Finally they found Monk Gotama at the village called *Uruvela Senanigom*, where he was staying at that time. They then came to wait on him in the hope that he would teach and help them reach the ultimate goal of enlightenment after he had achieved it himself. Those ascetics' names are *Konthañña, Vappa, Bhaddiya, Mahanama,* and *Assaji*. But when they witnessed his total renunciation of self-mortification, they became completely disappointed and left him for good. As for Monk Gotama, he realized undoubtedly that what he did was right, and that his new discovery of the middle path was a perfect way, which would certainly lead him to materializing his objective. So, the fact that those five ascetics abandoned him did not bother him at all. He moved forward pursuing his genuine practice with invincible perseverance and sheer spirit of intelligence.

In the night prior to that of his enlightenment he had five vivid dreams as follows:

1. He dreamt that he was lying on earth with his back on the ground and his mouth toward the sky while his head was lying on the Himalaya Mountain. In addition, his left hand dived deep into a great ocean in the western direction and simultaneously his right hand and both feet submerged in another boundless ocean in the southern direction.

He interpreted that dream as a clear indication that full enlightenment is inevitable and Buddhahood is within reach.

2. His second dream was concerned with a reed, which grew out of his navel and rose high up to the sky.

He understood such a dream as telling him about the fact that he would spread Dharma and teach a unique path to enlightenment and realization of nirvana.

3. He dreamt of uncountable worms, some were of black color, others of color white. They were climbing from both of his feet and filling up his shins and ending up at his knees.

This dream made him realize that millions of lay people as well as of Brahmans would enter his path and join in with him as regards the practice and realization of Truth.

4. Four flocks of birds with various colors such as yellow, green, red, and black flew from four directions and lighted on his two feet, then all of them became white.

He discerned lucidly the meaning of that dream which pointed to four classes of monarchs, brahmins, business people, and working class citizens who would join in with him regarding the practice and realization of Truth.

5. He dreamt that he ascended to perform his mindful walking meditation on a high mountain filled with shit, but they did not make his feet dirty even slightly.

The dream meant to say to him that he would not become somewhat attached to reputation, honor, and material gains received from those respecting and worshipping him.

Upon waking up he went through those dreams with pure mindfulness and impeccable awareness and fathomed their meanings remarkably. As a result, his heart was filled with great joy and upliftingly elated since there was no doubt whatsoever in his mind that what he had been searching for was awaiting his tender embrace right at the corner of Bodhi Tree (the Tree of Knowledge and Enlightened Wisdom).

Mudra 5

Mudra 5

Mudra of Receiving Madhupâyâsa

In this mudra the Buddha was seated in the samadhi posture with both palms opened and extended to the front. It is the mudra of receiving Madhupâyâsa (a most delicate meal particularly prepared with rich and abundantly nutritious ingredients). The illustrating story of this mudra is included in the mudra number 7 called *"mudra of throwing or letting a tray float against the current"*.

Mudra 6

Mudra 6

Mudra of Eating Madhupâyâsa

In this mudra the Buddha seated himself in the samadhi posture with his left hand holding the Madhupâyâsa tray while his right hand was positioned above its open space (mouth) showing the fingers in such a way that a lump of food was being picked up (the traditional Indian way of eating with one's hand). The illustrating story of this mudra is also included in the mudra number 7.

Mudra 7

Mudra 7

Mudra of Letting a Gold Tray Float on the Water

In this mudra the Buddha was seated in the sitting posture with his knees bent and resting on the ground (kneeling). His left hand was placed on his left thigh for maintaining the body perfectly erect while his eyes were cast down, with his right hand holding up the tray in a manner of placing it on the water.

Illustrating Story:

In uruvela senanigom village, not so far from where Monk Gotama was staying, there lived a wealthy man who had only a daughter named **Sujâta.** She had made a particular offering to a large bayan tree asking for a great husband and a handsome son as her first child. Some time later, her wishes were fulfilled, so following the tradition, she prepared a specific, neat food, specially cooked with all the ingredients of best quality for presenting it to a deva who, she believed, lived on that particular tree.

Therefore, on the full moon day of May she gave an order to her servants to arrange on a gold tray such a distinctive food called *Madhupâyâsa,* Then, that particular morning she carried on her head the Madhupâyâsa gold tray covered with another gold one and wrapped up with a very fine, fresh cloth, and together with her servants went directly to the bayan tree. There she saw the monk Gotama sitting under the tree with his face to the east, in a composed and dignified posture and with radiant lights shining forth. She then took it for granted that the deva (shining being) was awaiting her arrival with her promised offering.

Approaching him she presented him with high respect the gold trays of Madhupâyâsa, and the monk Gotama received them with his two hands. Since he could not find his bowl for keeping that specific food he looked at her with a gesture of letting her know that his bowl disappeared, and that he had nothing else to replace her gold trays. Understanding the meaning of his gesture, she wittingly said to him that she offered him those two gold trays as well. After that, she paid respect to him and took leave of him.

As for the monk Gotama, he then carried the Madhupâyâsa trays to Neranjará River that was running through the area near the Bodhi tree under which he was meditating. Then and there he seated himself on its bank facing the east, holding the Madhupâyâsa tray with his left hand, and made forty-nine lumps out of the Madhupâyâsa with his right hand. He ate all of them mindfully and meditatively. Thereafter, he took the gold tray to the river, and upon arrival at a small, lovely beach, he knelt on the ground with his left hand placed on his left thigh to keep his physical body erect while his right hand was putting the tray on the current of the river. Then, he made this wish: *If he would be blessed to reach enlightenment and become a Buddha, let the tray run against the current.* Immediately after that, he let the tray go out of his hand and float along Neranjará River. At that moment, with the power of all the good things he had done on Earth and the specific empowerment of his meditation there occurred a miracle. The gold tray ran against the current for a meter or so, and then sank into deep water.

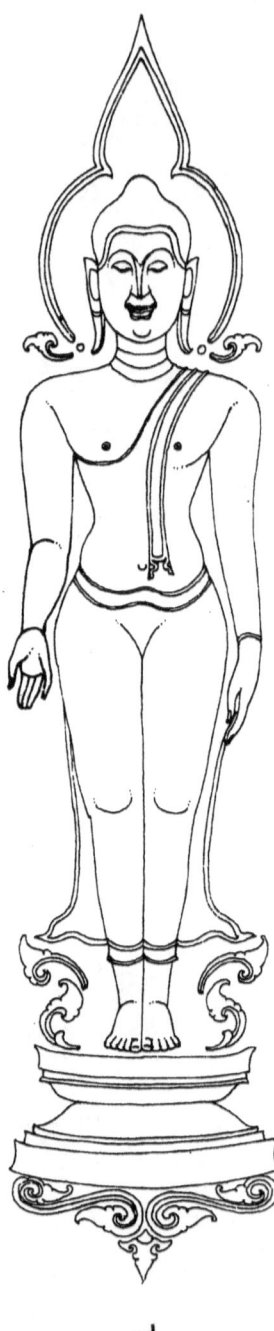

Mudra 8

Mudra 8

Mudra of Receiving Kusa Grass

In this mudra the Buddha was in the standing posture with his left hand hanging alongside the body while his right hand extended to the front with an open palm. This indicated his manner of receiving the kusa (sharply pointed-leafed) grass offered to him by a brahman named Sotthiya. The illustrating story of this mudra is included in that of mudra number 9 with its full story.

Mudra 9

Mudra 9

Mudra of Conquering Mâra

In this mudra the Buddha was seated in the samadhi posture with his left hand opened up and his right hand placed on his right knee with his fingers pointing to the earth. Regarding this mudra, some Buddhist artists began to add radiant lights shining forth from his head.

Illustrating Story:

The story goes like this: In the evening prior to his enlightenment the Buddha-to-be, the Monk Gautama, as he was called before becoming Buddha, had made an absolutely clear decision to fulfill his ultimate goal of Buddhahood, no matter what would happen. That particular evening a brahman named Sotthiya, who was making a living by cutting and selling Kusa grass (a kind of grass with sharp blades), offered to him eight bunches of this grass. Gotama made them into his meditation seat together with a cushion and began his intensive practice once and for all. During the night, Vasavatti Mâra, hearing this news, became terribly disturbed. He confronted the Monk Gotama, and demanded that the grass be returned, claiming to be its proprietor. The Monk Gotama refused this demand, and then Vasavatti Mâra moved his armed forces to fight and to destroy the monk Gotama. It is said that when Mâra's forces surrounded the Bodhi tree (tree of wisdom)[6] and were ready to fire at the Buddha-to-be, the personification of Mother Earth

---

[6] This Bodhi tree, sometimes written as Bo tree, has another name, Asattha, which means a fig tree. Close to the River Neranjarâ there was a fig trees grove where Monk Gotama spent his morning and early afternoon resting and absorbing a lovely, soft, and vital energy in its surroundings before he returned to the Bodhi tree for a big but gentle push for enlightenment.

(Dharanî), Vasundarâ by name, appeared in response to Monk Gotama's request for her help as a witness to all his ten perfections (paramitas) performed on Earth. She squeezed the water from her magical long black hair. The water flowed from the vicinity of the Kusa grass seat, and the land surrounding the Bodhi tree was flooded so deeply that all of Mâra's soldiers and their weapons were entirely submerged in water. No one was left alive, and Mâra was defeated once again.

Mudra 10

Mudra 10

Mudra of Enlightenment

In this mudra the Buddha was seated in the samadhi posture with both hands with palms up lying on top of each other. The right hand is placed on the left hand with the thumbs touching each other gently.

Illustrating Story:

After Monk Gotama had conquered the Mâra and its armed forces, with weapons of dharma paramitas he became extraordinarily elated. This great joy supported and uplifted both his physical and mental forces so that he could go on practicing Vipassana Meditation (cultivating and developing insight and wisdom) using ánápánasati (mindfulness with breathing) as the strong basis and solid foundation for Vipassana Practice. He did it to his utmost all night long without getting up from the samadhi posture. Then and there be became fully enlightened at the dawn of the day with the sun rising and darkness disappearing.

His enlightenment consists of three principal factors. The first factor is the vivid memory of his detailed past lives, which explode to him at the first watch of the night (around 10 p.m.). The second factor involves the visionary insights into birth, death and rebirth of all beings in the universe arising in him, at the second watch of the night (around 2 a.m.). The third factor is *Inner Knowledge and Insightful Wisdom* concerning all the defilements and contaminations within his consciousness that have been fully purified and totally transformed with no destructive elements left unfinished, arising in him at the last watch of the night (around 6 a.m.).[7]

In actual fact, the moment he became fully awakened to the Noble Truths and from the psychological and spiritual forms of sleep or reached enlightenment, five significant things rose in him; they are: Awakened Eye of Seeing things as they are (cakkhu), Insight or Profound Inner Vision (ñâna), All-Knowing Wisdom (paññâ), Illimitable and Illuminating Knowledge (vijjâ), and Unbounded Light (âloka). Together with those five factors he experientially realized the Four Noble Truths, namely, Suffering, Arising of Suffering, Cessation of Suffering, and the Middle Path[8] that leads to the Cessation of Suffering, which is the Realization of Nirvana. Finally, he exclaimed that his immeasurable Freedom, Full Awakening, and Realization of Nirvana are irreversible, the Holy (Whole) Life has been fully lived, all needs to be done has been done, and there is no more to do (the life's journey is completed).

---

[7] It was said in Pali literature that at the moment of Monk Gotama's enlightenment there occurred a miracle, that is to say, the entire Planet Earth was trembling, all trees and plants burst into blossoming, and all devas and brahmas both on the ground and in the sky were up roaring and expressing their overwhelming empathetic joy over his great success in becoming a Buddha. They all exclaimed in one voice: Buddha has arisen in the world just like the bright sun emerges and gives light to Earth.

[8] The Buddha's Middle Path consists of Eight Factors, namely, Perfect Wisdom or Right Understanding and Right Thinking (wisdom group); Right Action, Right Speech, and Right Livelihood (ethics group); Invincible Perseverance, Impeccable Mindfulness, and Right Focused Concentration or Firmly Stabilized Mind technically known as Samadhi (meditation group).

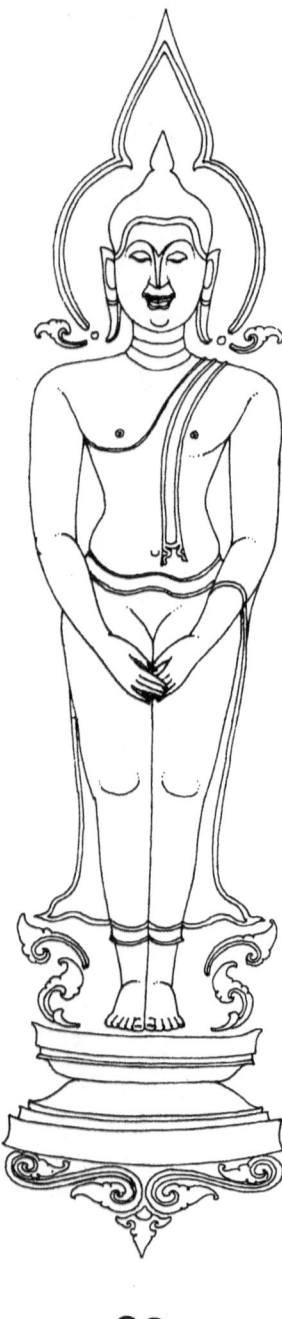

Mudra 11

Mudra 11

Mudra of Offering Eyes

In this mudra the Buddha was in the standing posture with both hands slightly raised and formed the overwrapping of one over another in front of his upper thighs, with his eyes wide open gazing steadily and intently at the Bodhi tree. The right hand was humbly placed over the left hand signifying the manner of self-control.

Illustrating Story:

After having reached enlightenment the Buddha spent seven days assimilating and enjoying the fruition of immeasurable freedom (vimuttisukha), which is the history of the Buddha image or Mudra of Achieving Enlightenment (Mudra 10). Right after that, he left the shade of the Bodhi Tree and went to take up a standing posture in an open space in the Northeast of the sacred tree, gazing intently and steadfastly at it without blinking his eyes for seven days. The place where he was standing became historically known as a blessed omen called **"*animisacetiya*"**. The Buddha's behavioral conduct of standing still and gazing steadily at the Bodhi Tree for such a long period of time inspired those Buddhist artists to build the Buddha image of " *offering his watchful eyes as a deep gratitude toward the Bodhi Tree*".

Those born on Sunday respectfully use this Buddha image for worship.

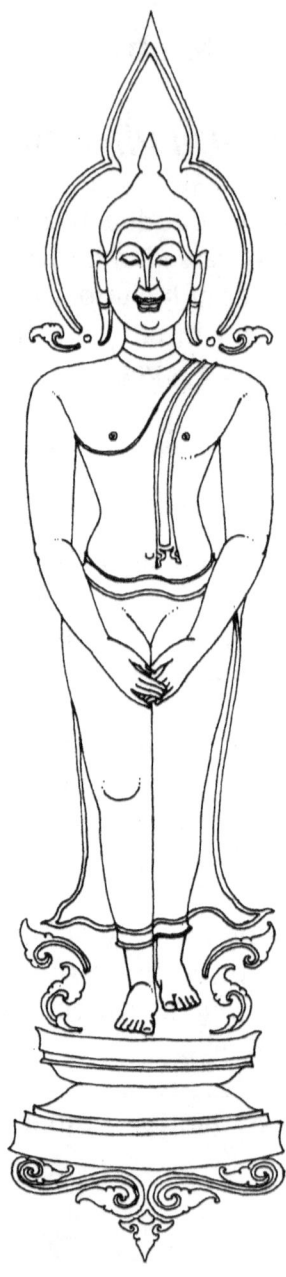

Mudra 12

Mudra 12

Mudra of A Sacred Mindful Walking

In this mudra, the Buddha was in the standing posture with his right foot placed on the ground while raising the heel of his left foot and positioning its toes on the earth. This implies a sacred mindful walking (cangamana) with both hands running alongside of his body and resting on his upper thighs in the form of wrapping one over another. His eyes were cast down and focused on the frontal space while he maintained mindfulness well established and unwaveringly steady. This is a meditative way of walking, which is executed alternately with sitting meditation.

Illustrating Story:

After he had done such a humble offering of his mindfully gazing eyes without blinking for seven days, he then left animisacetiya for a place located between the sacred Bo tree and the animisacetiya. There he was performing the sacred mindful walking for another period of seven days, which was the third week after his perfect enlightenment. Such a walk is technically known as *a sacred mindful walking*.

That cangamana which denotes the way by which a sacred mindful walking meditation is carried out, actually refers to the act of *pacing up and down* from one fixed place to another. Nowadays, we practice this kind of walking in a group by walking in a circle following after one and another, or walking individually in an open space in the field.

Mudra 13

Mudra 13

Mudra of Sitting in A Crystal House

In this mudra, the Buddha was seated in the samadhi posture in a crystal house (an entire cottage made of crystals) with both hands open and placed on top of one another, resting on his lap. In some places the Buddha image was made in such a way that the Buddha was sitting in a full lotus posture (with both feet on top of one another, traditionally called "diamond samadhi").

Illustrating Story:

After performing the sacred mindful walking for seven days, he left the cangamana Cetiya for another place in the northwestern direction of of the Bodhi tree, and there he seated himself in the samadhi posture inside the crystal house, investigating for seven days *Abhidharma*, the higher teaching, which consists of philosophy and depth psychology. The sacred place for establishing the crystal house is called "*Ratana Cetiya*".

His behavioral conduct of investigating and examining the *Abhidharma* in the *Ratana Cetiya* (crystal house) gave its name to that house. After seven days of the Abhidharma investigation he left it and went to the goatherd tree technically known as *ajapâla-nigrodha,* which was situated in the east of the Bodhi tree for continuation of taking delight in the fruition of immeasurable freedom.

At that time, a brahman who was strongly influenced by the habitual behavior of threatening others with nasty, rude words approached him and asked him this question: Bhaddante (blessed) Gautama, What kind of dharma(s) have been possessed by a person deserving to be called "brâhmana"? To that question Gautama the Buddha replied with great clarity thus: *Any brâhmana who has eradicated all evil, is utterly free from contaminations of all kinds, has had himself well controlled, endowed with vedic knowledge, and fulfilled the noble life of dharma and discipline, indeed deserves to be called* **brâhmana** through Dharma.

Mudra 14

Mudra 14

Mudra of Protection by a Serpent

In this mudra the Buddha was seated in the samadhi posture with both palms open and placed on top of one another, resting on his lap. Coiled around his physical body was a large serpent (nága) that multiplied his hood and head into seven and spread them all over the Buddha's head like a big umbrella to protect him from a heavy rainstorm and poisonous insects. Sometimes we witness this kind of Buddha image in the diamond samadhi posture.

Illustrating Story:

After seven days of taking delight in the immeasurable freedom under the ajapâla-nigrodha tree he then moved to another large tree named *mucilinda* located in southeast of the Bodhi tree and continued drinking up the above-mentioned emancipation. At that time it was raining continuously for seven days from a strong rainstorm. A huge serpent also called **Mucilinda** emerged from the kingdom of nâgas to protect the Buddha so that the rain would not touch and wet his body and to protect him from harm from those poisonous reptiles and insects. Jn so doing, Muccilind, Great King of nâgas, coiled around the Buddha's body and spread over his head his seven multiplied hoods and heads just as a large umbrella was firmly and securely set up for preventing rain. In this way, the Buddha could remain in his profound samadhi without any disturbances and therefore continued appreciating peace and bliss from the immeasurable freedom originally achieved under the Bodhi tree some seven weeks earlier.

After the rainstorm subsided and the rain stopped completely, Nâga Mucilinda released himself from the Buddha's body and returned to his normal state. Soon after that he disguised himself as a young man and appeared in front of the Buddha humbly paying him a revered respect in silence. Then and there the Blessed One uttered the following wise words:

> *Serene solitude is an authentic happiness for those who listen to Dharma and discern all conditioned things undoubtedly. They neither disturb nor cause any harm to anyone, instead embrace all beings with illimitable mettâ or universal love. They have liberated themselves from attachment to sensual pleasures and remain untouched by vicissitudes of life such as loss and gain, fame and defames, praise and blame, and so forth. Above all, they are so free from egoism and ego states that real happiness and true freedom accompany them just as (physical) shadow never leaves.*

Mudra 15

Mudra 15

Mudra of Consuming a Divine Fruit Called Samoh

In this mudra the Buddha was seated in the samadhi posture with his left hand open and placed on his lap while his right hand was rested on the right knee with open palm, holding a samoh (divine fruit). This indicates his manner of eating that special fruit.

Illustrating Story:

After spending seven days under the mucilinda tree appreciating deeply and drinking in thoroughly the fruition of enlightenment, which is the bliss of utter emancipation, the Buddha further moved to the râjâyatana tree (in Thai language, ketu) located in the south of the Bodhi tree. And after seven days he emerged from the samadhi vihâra (dwelling place) built on that spot. At that time the head god Indra thought to himself that the Buddha had spent seven weeks or forty-nine days in various places in the vicinity of the Bodhi tree since his full enlightenment, but had not eaten anything yet. So, he (Indra) brought with him a divine samoh, which was a nutritious, medical supplement (dibya osatha) and offered it to the Buddha. The latter received it and ate it in accordance with Indra's wishes. After that, he washed his mouth and cleaned his entire body, feeling at ease and wellbeing throughout his physiological components. He then remained there (under the râjâyatana tree for his last seven days).

For the above-described reason, the mudra of consuming a divine fruit is known in Thai language as samoh.

Mudra 16

Mudra 16

Mudra of Wrapping up His Alms-Bowl

In this mudra the Buddha was seated in the samadhi posture with his left hand holding a monk's alms-bowl that was placed on his lap while he raised his right hand above the bowl in a manner of closing it up. This indicates a way of wrapping up his alms-bowl.

Illustrating Story:

At the time when the Newly Enlightened Buddha was still staying at uruvela senanigama there were two merchants named *Tapussa and Bhallika* with their caravans of carts carried by oxen, which loaded all kinds of goods were passing through forest after forest from the *ukkala country*. At one point on their trips a deva whispered in their ears that a Buddha arose in the world and was residing under the râjâyatana tree, so they became extremely excited about the news and wanted very much to see him. Approaching the district where the Buddha was staying, they became absolutely alert and exceedingly aware, looking to the left, to the right, and all around. Soon after that, they saw him sitting in the samadhi posture under that particular tree. They then stopped their caravans and went to pay respect to him, bringing with them some barley meals in form of both flour and lumps and presenting them to him with a hope that he would eat them and therefore they (merchants) would gain a great deal of merit and blessings.

As a matter of fact, since he became the Buddha, he had never received any food offering from anyone. He then decided to receive from those two merchants their barley meals of both forms, allowing them to put such food in his alms-bowl (in Pali, patta). Here it's interesting to note that each Buddhist monk is allowed to possess only one alms-bowl, which indicates a life of contentment with having just a few or self-sufficiency without luxury whatsoever.

Mudra 17

Mudra 17

Mudra of Receiving Barley Meals

In this mudra the Buddha was seated in the samadhi posture with both hands holding his alms-bowl placed on his lap and with his eyes cast down. This shows the manner of receiving the barley meals with his alms-bowl.

The illustrating story regarding this mudra is already included in the above-cited story.

Mudra 18

Mudra 18

Mudra of Touching His Hair

In this mudra the Buddha was seated in the samadhi posture with his left hand opened upward and placed on his lap while his right hand was raised and rested above his head. This indicates his manner of magically touching his hair.

Illustrating Story:

After the Buddha had eaten their barley meals both Tapussa and Bhallika said to him thus: Blessed One! Both of us, from now on, take up the Buddha and his Dharma as our refuge. Therefore, let the Blessed Buddha recognize us as *upâsaka* in his religion from this moment until the end of our lives.

Then the Buddha, out of compassion and universal love, raised his right hand above his head and was rubbing his hair in such a way that eight pieces of hair came out with his hand. This is popularly known in Buddhism as *"element of magical hair"*[9]. He then gave them all to those two merchants, which they humbly received with their high respect. After that, they took leave of him and went their way back home.

It is worthy noting that those merchants, tapussa and bhallika by names, became the first upâsaka (the ones very close to the Buddha and the Dharma by going to them for refuge)[10]. Upon arrival home they built a sathupa for containing those

---

[9] In Pali, kesadhâtu.
[10] At the time when tapussa and bhallika took refuge, there was no Buddhist monk yet. So, they could have only Buddha and Dharma for their refuge, Normally, anyone wishing to become a Buddhist would be required to take refuge in tiratana (three Gems), namely, Buddha, Dharma, and Sangha.

eight pieces of the Buddha's hair as a monument of worship for all kinds of people and as a recollection of him (Buddhânussati).

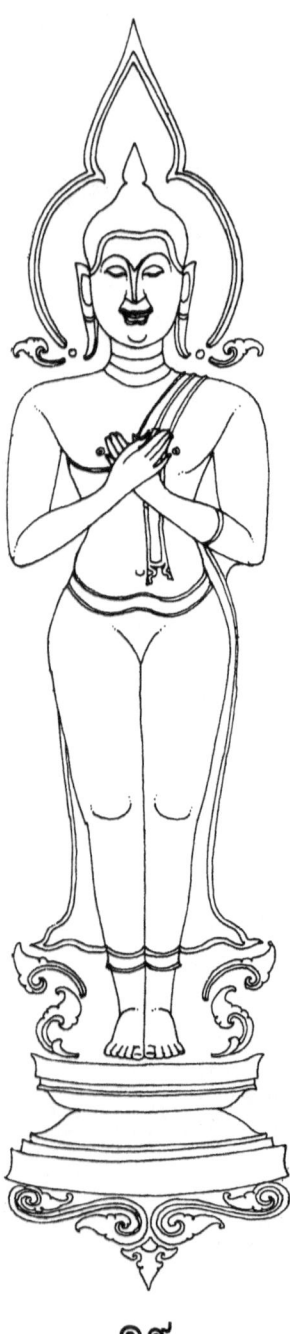

Mudra 19

Mudra 19

Mudra of Contemplative Reviewing

In this mudra the Buddha was in the standing posture with both hands overwrapping each other and placed on his chest. The right hand is resting on top of the left hand, which indicates a specific manner of contemplation and reviewing. In a variation, the Buddha was shown sitting in the samadhi posture.

In Thailand this mudra of the Buddha image is enthusiastically made for worship for those born on Friday.

Illustrating Story:

After Tapussa and Bhallika left, the Buddha moved away from the râjâyatana tree to the ajapâla-nigrodha tree and stayed under its shade once more. At that second time his heart and mind tended to contemplate and review the Dharma that he had realized through such a perfect enlightenment, seeing so clearly that it was subtle, profound, and fathomless that it would be extremely hard for anyone to understand and discern it. Such a contemplative review made him feel exceedingly discouraged that he thought of not teaching it to the public.

At that time a brahma, Sahampati by name (personified compassion) knew of the Buddha's thought and therefore announced it to all brahmas and devas, and asked them all to approach him (Buddha) together at the ajapâla-nigrodha tree. After exchanging their respectful greetings, they humbly requested that Blessed Buddha impart to innumerable and countless people the most valuable teachings (saddharma) that he experientially realized so that those who had just few dust (delusion and ignorance) in their eyes and dirt (contaminations) in their psychosomatic systems could attain to enlightenment and put an end to suffering.

Having heard such compassionate voices uttered by so-called sahampati and his fellow brahmas and devas he was reviewing and contemplating on the way by which what the previous Buddhas had done, and realized that they all taught their dharmas for the good, the welfare, and the benefit of those who had eyes to see, minds to understand, and hearts to take in those profound dharmas. With such realization he took up a definite decision to share with all beings his perfect knowledge and priceless experiences.

In addition, through his contemplation and review he saw clearly and unquestionably that there are four categories of people with their differentiated characters and potentials. They are: *First category* refers to those who are very ripe and quite mature, ready to realize the truth and to become enlightened upon hearing the Dharma; *second category* belongs to those who are about to get ripe and become mature, and would attain to enlightenment and realize the truth after listening to a few dharma talks; *third category* denotes those who would be teachable, advisable, and trainable, and after receiving an adequate training in dharma (meditation) and in ethical conduct (discipline regarding action and speech) could achieve the Eye of Truth (dharma-cakkhu) and be blessed with enlightenment and delighted in nirvana; whilst *fourth category* would remain in darkness and stay far away from light for a certain lifetime due to so much dust in their eyes and plentiful dirt in their body-mind constituents[11].

He then made a distinct comparison thus: The first type of people is compared to a lotus emerging from the water and staying above it, ready to open up as soon as it receives the sun. The second type is compared to a lotus reaching the surface of the water but still submerged inside it and waiting for a few days to rise above it. As soon as the sun shines on it, such a lotus

---

[11] 1. Vipatitaññû, 2. Uggatitaññû, 3. Neyya, and 4. Padaparama.

will bloom. The third type would be compared to a lotus living in the mid-water and taking a considerable time for growth before reaching the surface and rising above the water so that it would receive the sun, and then become fully blossomed. Only the fourth type is uncertain and inconvertible since they are like those lotuses that are covered with mud, which could become preys of fishes and turtles.

Those insights into the truth as regards the people in his time pushed the Newly Enlightened Buddha to vigorously teach and spread the Dharma to people of all walks of life with no discrimination whatsoever. In so doing, he helped millions and millions accomplish the goal of immeasurable freedom and liberate themselves as well as others from suffering, and appreciate deeply the elixir of enlightenment and unsurpassed peace of nirvana.

Mudra 20

Mudra 20

Mudra of Delivering First Discourse

In this mudra the Buddha was seated in the samadhi posture with his right hand raised to his chest and fingers formed in a circle pointing to the front while his open left hand is placed on his lap. This is the indication of his way of delivering a discourse or giving a dharma talk in general.

Illustrating Story:

When the Buddha was convinced to impart the dharma discovered under the Bodhi tree through his perfect enlightenment, he was then looking for those with mature faculties ready for listening to such profound dharmas. Then those two distinguished masters of his: Âlâra Kálámà and Udaka Râmaputta appeared in his thought, but at the same time he realized that they were both just recently dead. Continuing his search for the others who would be well prepared for giving their ears to his newly found dharmas, those five ascetics came to his mind in such a way that they were the first ones to receive his subtle and deep dharmas. After that, he set off his journey by foot directly heading toward *Isipatana migadâyavana* (Deer Park) in Benares where they were staying in accordance with his inner vision.

At first those ascetics did not believe in the enlightenment of the Buddha as he claimed to them. They poimted out to him that he had given up the severe practice of self-mortification and turned into becoming a luxurious monk by normally eating food as other unrestricted recluses did. So, it would have been impossible for him to become a Buddha since self-mortification was, according to their belief system, the only way to Enlightenment and Buddhahood.

The Buddha then reminded them of his statement which he had ever proclaimed before: "I am enlightened (or have become sabbaññu)." Upon realizing that he had never made such a statement to them or to anyone before, they decided to give him a chance to deliver his discourse to them to which they listened attentively and with respect. That discourse which he first delivered to those five ascetics is known as *dhammacakkappavattana* (setting in motion the wheel of Dharma in the irreversible way). In his first discourse the Buddha pointed out and made absolutely clear to them those two extreme practices as useless, unprofitable, and low graded. These two were self-mortification and self-indulgence in sensual pleasures: the former belongs to an extreme spiritualism while the latter is another extreme pathway of materialism. Right after delivering such an uproaringly brave statement he expounded his *middle path* that he just discovered and realized experientially. He further pointed out to them that his middle path is the genuine, authentic, and unique path that leads to everlasting peace, to perfect knowledge, to true enlightenment, and to realization of nirvana, whilst those two extreme paths are just the opposite, being conducive to a useless end, to low-graded involvements, and are not ways either to enlightenment or to heartfelt realization of Truth (Dharma).

In brief, let me cite to you, my reader, those eight factors which form the Buddha's Middle Path: They are **Right (perfect) Understanding, Right Thought, Right Action, Right Speech, Right Livelihood, Right Perseverance, Right Mindfulness, and Right Samadhi** (firmly and solidly stabilized mind or attentive absorption)[12].

---

[12] See *details* in same author's book, *Nirvana Upside Down*, ch.8, pages 211, published by Wisdom Moon Publishing, LLC, 2012

Mudra 21

Mudra 21

Mudra of Granting First Ordination

In this mudra the Buddha was seated in the samadhi posture with his left hand open and placed on his left knee while his right hand raised up with the palm facing the front and the fingers slightly bent. Such a performance indicated a welcoming or beckoning gesture.

Illustrating Story:

After Konthañña became initially enlightened, reaching the *stream of nirvana* technically known as *sotapanna* (attainment of irreversible flow), he requested an ordination for becoming a monk in Buddha's Dharma and Vinaya (Teaching and Discipline). Responding to his sincere request the Buddha bestowed upon him the first ordination, calling *"ehi bhikkhu"*, meaning "come on in and be a monk". The full text of that ordination goes thus: *Come on in and become a monk. Dharma has been well proclaimed by me. Practice the noble, chaste life for the purpose of putting an end to suffering."* With such a simple and brief statement Konthañña completed his ordination procedure and turned out to be the first Buddhist monk, following the Buddha, his Blessed Master.

Such first ordination initiated by the Buddha is known in Buddhism as ehibhikkhu upasampadâ (ordination by only beckoning and pronouncing monkhood). In that case the Buddha himself became the first, particular preceptor (upajjhâya). Because of such performance regarding the ordination, the mudra of granting or bestowing ehibhikkhu was made up with such an appropriate name.

The following day after the first sermon delivered to those five ascetics, the Buddha give some variety of instructions in meditation and dharma practice to the four remaining ascetics, namely, Bhaddiya, Vappa, Mahanama, and Assaji, and they all achieved the sotapanna enlightenment. Then and there in the Deer park the Buddha gave them the ehibhikkhu ordination so that they joined in his Order of Monks (bhikkhu parisâ). Soon afterward the Buddha delivered to his five bhikkhus (monks) the second significant discourse called *anattalakkhana suttanta;* and at the end of that discourse all those five newly ordained bhikkhus accomplished *full enlightenment.* By then altogether they were six perfectly enlightened bhikkhus, including the Buddha, in his Dharma and Vinaya or Sâsana (Buddhasâsana in full name) and in the whole world of the Buddha epoch.

Mudra 22

Mudra 22

Mudra of Eating a Meal

In this mudra the Buddha was seated in the samadhi posture with his left hand holding the alms-bowl placed on his lap while his right hand was put inside his bowl. This indicates the way in which he was eating a meal.

Illustrating Story:

At the time of his stay at Isipatana migadâyavana or Deer park there was a young man, Yasa by name, a son of a wealthy family residing in baranasi (Benares) who suffered the worldly life. Actually, his parents loved him so much so that they entertained him with all sensual pleasures that anyone could find in the world, including three castles built for him to say in three seasons each: one for dry season, another for rainy season; and the third one for winter. In addition, his pleasurable entertainments include all kinds of live music, dances of various forms, and innumerable beautiful young women.

One night he went to bed before everyone else, and then woke up during the night. He happened to go to a big hall in his castle with lots of light still brightly
lit on. Then and there he saw all his young people sleeping and manifesting themselves in various ugly ways just like corps in a forest cemetery, which he had never seen before. As a result, he encountered an unbearable disgusting feeling looming up powerfully inside him; and therefore he exclaimed to himself thus: *Here it's a complicated and restless world. Here it's a bondage in which the many are caught.* Witnessing with his own eyes and feeling utterly disgusted the loathsome and unpleasurable side of the mundane life he got dressed and put his shoes on; and then left his luxurious castle and the city before dawn. At the same time he was saying out loud those

above-exclaimed statements repeatedly as he was walking away from home along the country road.

As a matter of fact, he did not know where he was heading. He was just walking leisurely and with no direction. Eventually, he was inwardly directed to the Deer park where the Buddha and his five enlightened monks were residing. At that time (early morning) the Buddha was doing his mindful walking, pacing up and down mindfully. He then heard Yasa's complaining voices clear and loud thus: *Here it's a complicating and restless world. Here it's a world of bondage where many are caught.* In response to him, the Buddha then uttered his contrary statements saying: *Here it's not complicated and not restless but peaceful and tranquil. Here there is no bondage but immeasurable freedom. Come in here, sit down, and I will teach you a dharma.* So, he went in and sat down in a proper place and in a respectful manner, awaiting the dharma to flow in his attentive ears.

Then the Buddha taught him five categories of simple dharma technically known as *anupubbikathâ* (gradual instruction). They are, generosity, benevolence, or free giving (dâna), ethical conduct (sîla), heavens (sagga), pleasure and pain regarding pleasures of senses together with their consequences (kâmâdînava), and benefit from renouncing the world (nekkhamma), followed by four noble truth[13] that he discovered through his full enlightenment. Upon hearing and listening with a complete and focused attention Yasa attained to sotapanna: *entry in eternal flow of nirvana or initial and irreversible enlightenment.*

---

[13] Dukkha (pain, suffering, and all conditioned states/things), samudya (arising of dukkha), nirodha (total extinction of dukkha, which is nirvana), and majjhimâ patipadâ or magga (the middle path that leads to ending the dukkha).

Soon after that, his father, the wealthy man from Baranasi, arrived at Isipatana since he and many others were searching for him (Yasa) in all possible places in four directions (east, west, north, and south). There he saw his son sitting humbly and respectfully in front of the Great Master of the three worlds (humans, devas, and brahmas), he was extremely delighted and at the same time perplexed (because of not knowing what to make out of such a scene). Then, the Buddha gave him a dharma talk on the same subject that he delivered to his son, Yasa; and at the end of the discourse, Yasa's father also achieved sotapanna and became equally enlightened just as his son had. Furthermore, Yasa, with hearing and listening for the second time to such a basic instruction in the practical dharma, reached full enlightenment, which is *arahattaship*.

Not knowing the fact that his son became perfectly enlightened, the wealthy father asked him to return home to relieve the pain and sorrow his wife, his mother, and many others who suffered because of his abandoning them. The Buddha then told him about Yasa's state of arahattaship, and that he could not return to live that worldly life which he lived before. At that moment Yasa requested that the Buddha give him an ordination for becoming a bhikkhu and joining in with his Order of Monks, which the Buddha did without hesitation. As for the father who became equally irreversibly enlightened, he asked to take refuge in tiratana: Buddha, Dharma, and Sangha; which was granted to him, and therefore he was the first *upâsaka* in Buddhasâsana. Right after that he invited the Buddha and six other bhikkhus (his son included) to go and have breakfast at his house, which he accepted in serene silence.

At Yasa's father's house, the Buddha instructed Yasa's mother and his former wife in anupubbikathâ and in the four noble truths as he previously did to Yasa and his father. Consequently, those women accomplished the initial and irreversible enlightenment known as sotapanna. They too joined in with the Buddha's parisâ and became the first *upâsikâs* in Buddhasâsana. Then it was breakfast time, so Yasa's father, his mother, and his former wife brought in the well and neatly prepared food to offer to him, which he received in his alms-bowl with appreciation in serene silence and ate it mindfully. It was the first meal that the Buddha ever ate at someone's house since his enlightenment, which is considered a highest blessing and an uppermost grace in Buddhism. For this reason, the Buddha image was created for signifying the mudra of eating a meal.

Mudra 23

Mudra 23

Mudra of Stopping his Relatives from Water Dispute

In this mudra the Buddha was in a standing posture with both of his hands raised to the level of his chest and with the palms opened and bent forward, indicating a sign to stop.

Illustrating Story:

After he converted Yasa into Buddha Dharma through his discourses on the gradual teachings and four noble truths, the Buddha helped Yasa's four friends, namely, Vimala, Subâhu, Punnaji, and Gavampati, by imparting the dharma until they accomplished enlightenment and got ordained into bhikkhu Sangha. In addition, he further converted fifty more friends of Yasa and gave them all ehibhikkhu ordination since they became perfectly enlightened. By then, there were sixty arahatta bhikkhus forming the Order of Enlightened Monks. The Buddha then considered it the right moment for dispatching them to teach and spread the dharma out of compassion for all beings and people of all walks of life, so he summoned them all and declared to them these incredible statements as follows:

"Monks! Now all of you and I have been liberated from all kinds of bondage and snares and have equally reached immeasurable freedom, go out to the world and present the dharma to all interested in it and ready for realization of truth. This is uniquely for benefit, for happiness, and for welfare of all human beings, devas, and brahmas without discrimination. To carry out this dharma mission do not go anywhere in two but alone, so that those having less dust in their eyes and less dirt in their body-mind systems but are mature with their faculties and meritorious deeds will benefit from our selfless and compassionate services. I also will go by myself to Uruvela district for preaching the dharma."

After dispatching all sixty arahatta monks to various parts of the world in Jambûdîpa (old India), the Buddha himself went to that Uruvela district of Magadha State which he had stated to his monks. On his way he encountered a party of young men, 30 in number, who were searching for a lost young woman. During his resting time by a cotton field, he inquired into what they were doing, and after getting informed precisely he expounded the dharma laying an emphasis on *the search for Self* as the most significant thing to do. Upon listening attentively to his discourse, those thirty noble young men got converted to the dharma through realization of truth and possession of *the all-seeing eye or the eye of wisdom*. In turn, the Buddha gave them ehibhikkhu ordination and then sent them all out to help all sentient beings just as he did with his other monks since they were all perfectly enlightened as well.

At Uruvela district there lived three brother ascetics called *jatila* (those ascetics who wear a braid of hair or have their hair matted). Their practice was *fire worship*. The Buddha deliberately went to take his residence in Uruvela Kassapa's ashram, the head of five hundred jatilas. Actually, he was highly revered and popularly respected by quite a number of populations in Magadha State, a strong hold of Brahmanism and Hinduism. That's why the Buddha chose that State to be a place for establishing his Dharma and Vinaya (Buddhasâsana). Since those jatila ascetics held in respect and worship quite a large number of followers, he (Buddha) made his choice to meet with a great challenge in laying down a solid foundation of his Sâsana (Religion in its true sense of Restoration); and he succeeded admirably. Those three jatila brothers and all their followers were converted into Buddhasâsana, and soon after that Bimbisara, Great King of Magadha (a Super Power State), was also convinced of the Buddha and his Dharma so that he became the Buddha's sâvaka (literally "hearer", but in general it means "follower") and a significant supporter of Buddhasâsana. In this way, we say that the Buddha had achieved a magnificent success in spreading his dharma and in establishing his Sâsana.

At one point, during his Dharma combat with Uruvela Kassapa at his private residence and ashram of fire worship, the Buddha demonstrated a miracle of stopping an unexpected flood miraculously invented by the head of jatilas. He (Buddha) was performing a mindful walking meditation in a place where the flood is heading to, but he prevented it from running through his place; instead, he let it flow around him, forming a wide stretch of water while he was walking mindfully amidst it just like an island emerging in the middle of the sea. Those three jatila brothers sailed their boats along such a huge flood watching the Buddha in his walking posture astonishingly. Because of this miracle performance those who are enthusiastic about it had this same mudra made up and called it "a *mudra of preventing the miraculous sea of flood*".

Let us return to our illustrating story of the mudra of stopping his relatives from water dispute (war). Historically speaking, there existed two capital cities: one belonging to Sakyans, his relatives on his father side, called "Kapilavatthu"; another with the name of "Devadaha", which belonged to Koliyans, the Buddha's relatives on his mother's side. Those two cities were situated on each edge of Rohini River and depended on its waters for irrigation to provide water for their rice fields. In that particular year when the Buddha just started his Dharma Mission, there were droughts all over the regions of those two small kingdoms. So, peoples of both sides of the river needed some water for growing rice. At first they individually made their private irrigations and built some dams here and there to keep sufficient waters so that their rice fields could have enough supplies. This caused the original dispute since neither side had a sufficient supply of water as they needed. Later on, the dispute spread wide and far and eventually became a war superbly challenging the two kingdoms. Consequently, the troops of the

Sakyans and those of the Koliyans were deployed close to their riverbanks, preparing to fight one another.

Upon hearing about such a dispute, the Buddha decided to intervene, so he went over and mediated peace for his two beloved previous kingdoms. Arriving at the ready-to-combat-field he first held a peace talk with the military commanders of both Sakyan and Koliyan troops, and then had a joint meeting with those two Kings of the two kingdoms. After the friendly and compassionate conversations with them, he then put to them a very simple question: *What were more significant and most dear to you both: the blood of your peoples or the water?* Both Kings answered him in one voice: **Blood**. In this way, the war was cancelled and peace prevailed.

After the complete withdrawal of the troops the two kingdoms continued co-existing and cooperating in harmony, peace, and love, managing and sharing the waters from the Rohini river without much difficulty. Such a compassionate action taken by the Buddha regarding the water dispute between his relatives of two sides of the river was so reverently and deeply appreciated by Buddhists that the Buddha image of *"mudra of stopping his relatives from verging on water war"* was built for signifying and recollecting peace over war.

Mudra 24

Mudra 24

Mudra of Appointing two Great Disciples

In this mudra the Buddha was seated in the samadhi posture with his left hand opened up and placed on his lap while his right hand rose with the index finger pointing toward the front. This indicates his appointment of two great disciples (to the posts of his right and left hands).

Illustrating Story:

At that time there existed two young men who were good friends or buddies and playmates since their childhood. They were as known Upatissa and Kolita. They lived in the same village, attended to the same school for studying liberal arts and sciences, and above, all loved each other dearly. Being young and youthful, they spent their lives in the similar way as the young people of their ages did in their time, for example, going to cinema and to other entertainments.

One day in the middle of watching a movie they both felt strongly that it was useless and a waste of time seeing and watching all those artificial, superficial things invented and made up by those professionals who earned their living by writing scripts and making movies. So, they left the theatre during the movie and went to a quiet place for an intelligent discussion on the essence of life. Right after that, they were searching for a master who could help them reach the essential and transcend the inessential. Eventually they found Sañjaya paribbâjaka (wandering religious mendicant) who had a large ashram just outside of Râjagaha, the Capital City of Magadha State, and was teaching quite a number of followers. They went there and asked him to accept them as his disciples to become paribbâjakas, which he did with delight.

After being well trained and endowed with knowledge (a package of understanding and experience), they became teachers and helped their master teach many disciples (each of them had as many as two hundred fifty disciples). Nonetheless they both were not satisfied with what they had achieved through all the teachings and training techniques imparted to them by Sañjaya. For this reason, they made a mutual agreement that if one of them found something new and more appealing to their ultimate goal of life, let him tell the other before taking it up himself. Such an agreement was a commitment and indispensable matter for them both.

One early morning Upatissa paribbâjaka left the ashram and headed toward the city for no clear motif. He then had a glance of Assaji, a newly enlightened disciple of the Buddha walking along the city street so mindfully and with all his faculties in natural control and shining forth radiantly that he became quite amazed by such a sight. But realizing that the monk was collecting food from donors lining up in street he did not feel appropriate to approach him right away, and therefore he just followed Assaji in a proper distance until he had done his round.

Once monk Assaji had collected sufficient food for nourishing his physical body, he went out of the city to find a suitable place for having his meal. Then and there at the lovely and peaceful spot, Upatissa approached him and humbly asked him about his master and the teachings professed by him. Perceiving an obvious intelligence in Upatissa, monk Assaji replied to his questions by saying that he was just freshly ordained by the Buddha, his Great Master, so he would be unable to tell him much about his Master's teaching. Upon hearing his humble response, Upatissa requested that he only give him just a few words so that he could grasp the meaning and essence of the teaching. In that regard Assaji said these short sentences: *All things arise from causes, and my Great*

Master expounds them together with their cessations. With attentive listening to such a dharma (teaching), Upatissa got its meaning and essence, so he thanked monk Assaji deeply for his valuable statement of truth, and then asked him where the Buddha was residing. After receiving the address of the Master's residence, which was Veluvana monastery, he took his leave immediately since he had to tell his friend, Kolita paribbâjaka, before pursuing the new teaching conveyed to him by the enlightened monk Assaji.

After both noble friends, Upatissa and Kolita, met and discussed the new findings, they became exceedingly enthusiastic and therefore, headed toward the monastery to meet with the Buddha straightaway. Upon receiving more teaching directly from the Great Master, they asked for ordination to become bhikkhus and disciples of the Buddha, which he bestowed upon them instantaneously.

Seven complete days after becoming ordained and meditating intently and absorbedly in accordance with the Buddha's precise instructions Kolita (who after his ordination was known as Moggallana), accomplished perfect enlightenment. In the meantime Upatissa or Sariputta (as he was named after his ordination) achieved such enlightenment within fifteen days (one week more in comparison with his friend). They both assisted the Buddha in teaching disciples as well as in spreading the dharma with diligence, with power of wisdom and compassion, and with supernatural power in a dedicated and selfless form.

For the above-cited reasons the Buddha, on an auspicious day amidst joint assembly of his bhikkhus and bhikkhunis (female monks), appointed Sariputta, specialist in profound wisdom, to the Right Hand Disciple, while Moggallana, who was specialized in supernatural power of all forms, received the appointment to the Left Hand Disciple.

Mudra 25

Mudra 25

Mudra of Preaching His Principal Teachings

In this mudra the Buddha was seated in the samadhi posture with both hands raised to his chest level and all the fingers slightly crossed, which is similar to the mudra of descending from the Távatimsa heaven. Such an act indicates his manner of discoursing or giving a dharma talk.

Illustrating Story:

At one time the Buddha was seated amidst his enlightened monks, 1250 in number, who gathered together at Veluvana Monastery located in the outskirts of Rájagaha city. In that afternoon he preached the main principles of his Teaching (Dharma) technically called *ovâdapâtimokkha* to the great congregation. In such a congregation there happened simultaneously four categories: (1) those 1250 monks were all perfectly enlightened. (2) They all received ehibhikkhu ordination from the Buddha directly. (3) All of them happened to come to assemble at the Buddha's residence without any appointment whatsoever. (4) Such a magnificent day accidentally fell on the full moon day of March popularly known in Buddhism as *Mâgha-pûjâ*.

Here are those principal teachings, which he was preaching to such a great congregation:

Patience is that self-control (ability to remain calm), which is the effective dharma for burning away and cleansing off all contaminations/defilements (kilesa). The wise identify nirvana, the excellent dharma. Those harming or causing damage to others are not pubbajitas¹⁴/bhikkhus, nor are those who trouble or make somebody worried or upset recluses.

Not to commit any evil, but to do all that is good, and to purify one's mind (also to awaken one's heart): all these are teachings of the Buddhas.

Not to blame or speak spiteful words to anybody, not to do any harm to others, to be restrained in Dharma and Vinaya (Teaching and Discipline), to be moderate in consuming, taking a residence in a healthy, peaceful, and quiet environment, and persevering in purification and transformation of mind and heart. All these are teachings of all the Buddhas.

After laying out those major teachings to those 1250 enlightened monks, he urged them to continue making known to all sentient beings Buddhasâsana or Dharma and Vinaya out of compassion and with selfless service for the benefit, happiness, and welfare of them all without any discrimination.

---

[14] Those who have gone forth (into the holy life or pabbajâ).

Mudra 26

Mudra 26

Mudra of Sitting on the Boat

In this mudra the Buddha was sitting on a throne with both feet placed on a large, open lotus while both palms of his hands covered and resting on his thighs.

Illustrating Story:

At the time of his stay at Veluvana Monastery in the Great City of Râjagaha, the Buddha delivered many discourses and helped millions of those having few dust in their eyes realize the truth and become enlightened. He taught the dharma practices for beginners, intermediate, and advanced people respectively; and converted those having some wrong view and confusion to right understanding and right thinking that forms a wisdom group in his middle path. Furthermore, he expounded and pointed out clearly and precisely the Noble Eightfold Path that leads to realization of nirvana and to attainment to perfect enlightenment. In this way, countless number of people from all walks of life, including recluses (samana), wandering religious mendicants (paribbâjakas), devas and brahmas, turned to him for getting help to achieve liberation from contaminations, be they mental, psychological, or spiritual (or all of them), as well as to put an end to suffering once and for all. In short, he succeeded in establishing his Sâsana (Teaching and Discipline) in Super Power Magadha State ruled by the Righteous, Enlightened King, Bimbisara by name, his most significant supporter and follower.

During that period of time, Vesali, the great, capital city of Vajji State ruled by Licchavi monarchs, was richly prosperous and vastly developed with regard to education and economy. There were numerous investors, traders, bankers, and merchants carrying out their businesses all over that large city and its vicinity. In Vajji State, another Super Power State, natural resources were abundant and the land was extremely rich, and therefore the people of Vesali became especially wealthy with properties, money, and treasures of gold and silver, etc. Within Vesali itself, there existed quite a number of parks, botanical gardens, common gardens, and lovely, recreative places well and properly planned for all suitable parts of the city.

Unfortunately three big crises, namely, a crisis of *drought, a crisis regarding non-human beings (evil spirits and ghosts), and a crisis of deadly epidemic disease (***cholera***)*, fell on Vesali city and Vajji State as a whole. The people suffered their worst economic downfall in which consumption costs were extremely high and prices of consuming things for day-to-day living were soaring. In addition, countless numbers of poor and abandoned people who received no aid and caring whatsoever neither from City Administration nor from Government of State, died on streets of Vesali. So, many parts of that great city turned into a cemetery, so to speak. Since nobody including City Administration and Government took care of the dead, the corpses became rotten and the city streets were filled with human filth, mess, and mud nearly everywhere. Consequently, human-corpse-eating animals such as vultures, insects, reptiles, and innumerable flies, as well as so-called evil spirits and ghosts entered the city to join in with those ghosts of the dead inside, together with human-corpse-eating animals. These caused an epidemic, a deadly disease called "cholera", which spread rapidly all over Vesali city and its neighborhood. As a result, thousands and thousands of people abandoned and fled their city homes in search for proper places to live such as their neighboring State, and also in far away Countries. This inevitably turned out to be a refugee crisis!!

In response to those crises, the traditionally minded people of Vesali performed a variety of sacrifice offerings to guardian spirits and protective gods in the hope that a solution to the crises would be achieved. But all their performances were in vain. On the part of the Government, nothing effective got done for solving those terminal crises, although they attempted in all possible ways and means to do what they could. Also, all was in vain!!

Nonetheless, there were many Buddhists living and practicing Buddha Dharma in Vesali; they gathered together and selected those wise people from their community to go to the Licchavi Monarchs, Rulers of Vajji, and present to them their initiatives of inviting the Buddha to come over for solving those crises once and for all. After discussing thoroughly with his cabinet ministers and advisers the Buddhist initiatives for definitive solution, the Monarchs agreed to their proposal and gave the command to those involved with foreign affairs to carry out the extension of an invitation to the Buddha. Fortunately, Prince Mahali, the Crown Prince of Licchavi, got to know and had a close association with King Bimbisara, Ruler of Magadha State, who was the Buddha's genuine supporter. Without his approval, it would have been impossible to get the Buddha to Vesali to perform the healing and restoring work for their city. So, they appointed Mahali the principal envoy to head the Licchavi Monarchs' representatives. Consequently, Prince Mahali prepared his ambassadorial party and then left for Râjagaha, the Capital City of Magadha. Then and there, he presented to King Bimbisara an official letter from his Licchavi Monarchs, which was cordially accepted.

Since it was rainy season and close to Lent Observance (a three-month period for contemplation) for the Buddha and his monks, King Bimbisara approached the Master and asked if he would accept such an invitation to do something in his extraordinary power for helping and liberating Vesali from its deadly crises. As expected, the Buddha, after pondering such an important issue and perceiving clearly through his visionary insight that his trip to Vesali would ultimately help restore the city and rescue its citizens, and would therefore eradicate those three deadly crises completely, did accept it out of compassion and universal, mega love for the people of Vesali, the Capital City of Super Power Vajji.

Upon realizing that the Buddha would certainly travel to Vesali following the humble request from the Licchavi Monarchs, King Bimbisara requested that the Buddha wait for a little while since he had to prepare the walk path from Râjagaha to Ganges River to make it smooth and comfortable for traveling. Then he gave his royal command to the department of public road works to get the walk path ready as soon as possible so that the Buddha and his accompanying monks could travel by foot with ease and contentment. In addition, he ordered to have a large resting hall built every forty kilometers so that the Buddha and his five hundred monks would be able to rest and spend a night since the length of distance from his capital city to that part of Ganges River would be approximately two hundred kilometers. That means that the trip would take five days to reach the harbor wherefrom the royal ship would depart for Vesali, which would take a journal of about three full days.

When all the works had been done, King Bimbisara informed the Master of his thorough preparation for the Buddha's significant trip aimed at carrying out his Dharma Mission for the good, the benefit, and freedom from crises that confronted the people of Vesali. Then, the Great Master of the world set out his trip accompanied by the royal charioteer that carried King Bimbisara and his royal family while all the dignitaries and common people were on their feet following the Buddha's procession until he reached the royal harbor where the royal boat awaited his arrival. He then ascended on the well-prepared boat and seated himself on the ready-made throne surrounded by his five hundred monks and the group of six ambassadorial representatives headed by Prince Mahali from Vesali. After seeing the Buddha off, King Bimbisara and his loyal people returned home to Râjagaha City. Within three days the Buddha's party arrived at Vesali where the Licchavi Monarchs together with their Government ministers, advisers, dignitaries, and citizen from all walks of life were stationed with enthusiasm and excitement at the Ganges River's bank to welcome him with great honor and high respect. As a matter of fact, the boat trip took the Buddha three days to reach the frontier of Vajji State of which Vesali was the Capital. After terminating the warm and honorable welcome ceremony they were all leading the Buddha and his monks to their troubled city.

Upon setting his feet on the edge of Vesali, the Buddha stood still and looked up to the sky contemplating on rain for a short while. Soon after that the dark clouds gathered together and slowly moved down to the lower sky, creating powerful thunder and flashes of lightening everywhere above the ground. Then the heavy rain poured down, removing and cleaning away all the corpses, dirt, and dust from the streets and every corner of Vesali. Hearing the forcefully loud noises of the thunder and lightening, all the evil spirits, hungry ghosts, and poisonous animals fled for their lives and left the city with no hesitation. Consequently, the City of Vesali was miraculously liberated from its troubles, and then its entire citizen became safe, sound, and happy.

Furthermore, the Buddha instructed his attendant monk, Ananda, together with his five hundred monks to learn *Ratanasutta* and then chant it along all over the streets of Vesali. At the same time, Ananda, accompanied by the dignitaries and Government officials, holding his bowl filled with sacred water sprinkled it all over places as he passed by, and therefore those who were sick through the deadly disease of the cholera attack got healed and became well once again through such a meditative chanting and the highest power of the Buddha enhanced by a great many prodigious powers of those enlightened monks. When all had been done, he together with his fellow monks and those accompanying him returned to the Buddha and informed him of all the happenings. Then the Great Master of the world delivered his dharma talks for a period of three days to the countless number of Vesali people together with their Monarchs and their Government officials. (Actually, a lecture on dharma is equal to prescribing and taking sweet medicine so that a healing of illness and a health restoration could take place.) By such a transformative performance and creative presence of the Buddha, all the three deadly crises were utterly terminated. As a result, Vesali and all its Administration people as well as common citizens returned to wellbeing, prosperity, and affluence, as before.

After his Dharma Mission had been successfully completed the Buddha and his monks returned to Veluvana (Bamboo grove) Monastery in Râjagaha of Magadha State for spending their rainy season (Lent Observance: again, a three-month period for contemplation) there.

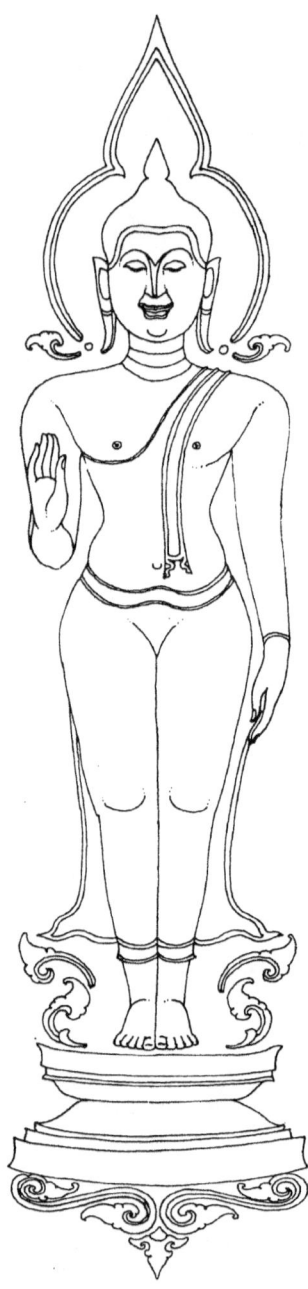

Mudra 27

Mudra 27

Mudra of Letting Diseases Discontinue

In this mudra the Buddhas was in a standing posture with his left hand hanging (stretching) down along side his body while his right hand rose up to his chest level with its open palm extending outward. This is the manner of prohibiting and/or preventing diseases.

Illustrating Story:

Details of this story are exactly the same as the previous one. So, you, my reader, may go back and reread the above-cited illustrating story.

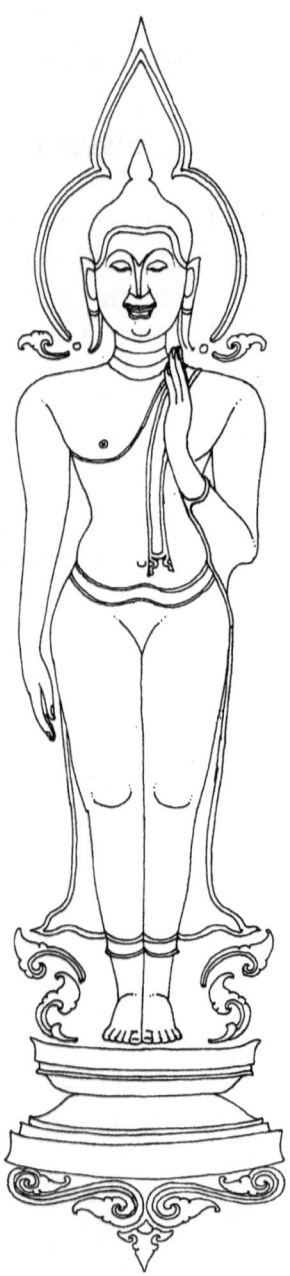

Mudra 28

Mudra 28

Mudra of Performing Supernatural Power

In this mudra the Buddha was in a standing posture with his left hand raised to his chest level and with its open palm facing toward the right side while his right hand hanging (stretching) down along side his body, resting near his right knee.

Illustrating Story:

At one time during his stay at Veluvana Monastery situated in the outskirts of Râjagaha, he would make his daily rounds for collecting alms-food, and also delivered discourses on Dharma regularly to those interested in fulfilling their spiritual developments, in reaching enlightenment, and in realizing nirvana. Included in those day-to-day activities were his fourfold parisâ, namely, bhikkhus, bhikkhunis, upâsakas, and upâsikâs.

When his father, King Suddhodana of Kapilavatthu, the Capital City of Sakyan Kingdom, knew of the Buddha's honor, fame, and prosperous, spiritual work for humanity spread widely all over the Super Power States such as Magadha and Vajji, he became exceedingly happy and highly proud of his son's success both in achieving his perfect enlightenment and in helping millions of people liberate themselves from suffering and accomplish their ultimate goals of immeasurable freedom and nirvana. Also, he was absolutely pleased to hear some good news that the Buddha was contemplating on a visit to his native kingdom and to his royal family at Kapilavatthu. He unhesitatingly dispatched a group of young princes who represented him to Veluvana Monastery for inviting the Buddha to pay a visit to him and his kingdom. Those in the group of envoys joined in with the Buddha's Order of Monks, and never uttered a word of invitation to the Great Master. King Suddhodana had done the dispatching of his representatives to Veluvana Monastery literally nine times, and they all became monks and never returned. So, the tenth time he considered to send Kâludâyi, his close aide, who was a great friend and was of the same age as Siddhattha[15], to invite the Buddha to visit him and his kingdom.

Before accepting the king's command, Kâludâyi requested that he permit him to join in with the Buddha's Order of Monks, a humble request King Suddhodana reluctantly granted him. So, Kâludâyi collected his good and noble people to accompany him, and then they set off their missionary journey. Upon arriving at Veluvana Monastery and listening to the Buddha's lucid discourse, they all asked for the ordination to join him in the monastic life, which the Buddha bestowed upon them. After eight days of ordination, Kâludâyi approached the Buddha and presented to him his father's invitation, which the Buddha accepted in serene silence. That was a great success on Kâludâyi's part and an utter happiness for King Suddhodana when he received the message that Kâludâyi sent to the king, informing him of the Buddha's visit to Kapilavatthu.

Upon the Buddha's arrival at the Sakyan Capital City together with his twenty thousand monks, his father and all his royal relatives gathered together for receiving him with a warm home welcoming. Needless to say how happy and highly elated they all were!! In this way, the Buddha reached his hometown with an honorable dignity (which he didn't really need but accepted in tranquil and appreciative silence).

Since his royal relatives including King Suddhodana were all infatuated with their royal pride and rigid view on things and on life, they thought that the Buddha was just their young man and junior to them in ranking status, so they did not relate to

---

[15] The Buddha's personal name when he was the prince.

him in a respectful, humble manner, as they should. Perceiving this kind of arrogance and self-aggrandizement, the Great Master of the world, out of compassion for them all, decided to demonstrate his impressive supernatural power so that they could reduce their monarchal pride and narrow-minded opinions, so that, in consequence, their hearts and minds would become more open and more awakened. For this very reason, he did show his supernatural power, which was rather rare except that the matter turned into the matter of death and life regarding the Dharma.

As for such a demonstration the Buddha simply elevated himself and flew up to the sky, and then seemingly let some dust from his feet fall down on the heads of those royal relatives present at the great gathering, including King Suddhodana's head. It was a miraculously astonished for them all.

Consequently, King Suddhodana together with those royal relatives and dignitaries surrendered them to the supreme power of the Buddha, and were prepared to listen to his dharma talks, which he did eloquently and eruditely. At the end of the Buddha's sermon, his father entered into nirvanic flow, and became initially enlightened while all others benefited enormously from his discourse on the dharma. Then, all of a sudden, an unexpected incident took place miraculously, and that was, a lotus-leaf rain[16] poured down heavily, in which those wanting to get wet were made wet while those who did not want to, did not become wet by such a miraculous rain. To clarify the matter, the Buddha told them that such a special rain came down to earth not only this time but at the time when he was

---

[16] In Pali, pokkhara-vassa — lotus-leaf rain, a portentous shower of rain serving as special kind of test rain to which certain objects are made wet, but those showing disinclination toward moisture are left untouched, like a lotus-leaf.

born Prince Vessantara[17], a bodhisatva, in one of his significant previous lives. Then and there he delivered another discourse on Vessantara Jâtaka (chronicle of Vessantara in Pali text).

---

[17] This Pali term (Vessa + antara = Vessantara) refers to that which is in between businessmen such as investors, traders, bankers, merchants, and so forth. It was said that Prince Vessantara was so named because of his birth in a Commercial District.

Mudra 29

Mudra 29

Mudra of Holding His Alms-Bowl

In this mudra the Buddha was in a standing posture with both feet joined tightly together on the ground while both hands held the alms-bowl placed at the level of his lower abdomen. This Buddha image is well known as *"mudra of holding his alms-bowl"*, and traditionally help to serve explicitly for worship for those born on Wednesday.

Illustrating Story:

At the time of his visit to Kapilavatthu, the Buddha at first demonstrated a supernatural power of flying up to the sky for subduing his royal relatives, and then magically caused the lotus-leaf rain to fall heavily on earth amidst those subdued relatives, and finally expounded a discourse on Vessantara Jâtaka laying an emphasis on *Perfection of Giving or Benevolence* (dâna paramita). At the end of his lucid and fluent dharma talk those present at the great assembly headed by his father, King Suddhodana, became highly elated with their hearts and minds filled with boundless joy and zest as already described in the previous story illustrating the mudra number 28.

After the gathering was over ,none of those royal relatives including the King of Kapilavatthu offered any invitation to the Buddha for having breakfast at their royal residences. They all thought that the Buddha would lead his monks to the royal palace of his father for having breakfast. That was their total ignorance since in the monastic tradition no monk would go to anybody's house without receiving an invitation. Since the Buddha followed the Buddhas' tradition strictly, when nobody invited him, the following morning he picked up his alms-bowl and led all his monks, each holding his alms-bowl in his hands, to the city street for collecting alms. A great number of people queued up along both sides of streets to behold him with great joy and enthusiastically offered him their neatly prepared food. It was the first time after he left them for becoming a monk and attaining Buddhahood, for the citizens of Kapilavatthu to see him holding his alms-bowl in his both hands and walking bare feet with grace and with his radiant faculties in lovely and respectful control. They were all indescribably very happy and immensely enriched receiving unexpectedly from him and his enlightened monks such soaring blessings.

Mudra 30

Mudra 30

Mudra of Teaching His Father

In this mudra the Buddha was in his standing posture with his left hand holding his alms-bowl while his right hand was raised with all his joint fingers slightly bent forward, indicating the manner of imparting the dharma.

Illustrating Story:

In the previous mudra story we described the Buddha's activity of going round in the Kapilavatthu streets for collecting alms and for helping people gain merit and receive his blessings; those common citizens who lined up on both sides of streets were extremely happy and enthusiastic in beholding him and in offering him their immaculately prepared food. Then, his father, King of Sakyan Kingdom, heard about such a behavior of his son, the Buddha. He felt very sad and disdainful since the monarch and his family members would have never done such a thing, meaning, begging for food on street. Therefore, he went straightaway to the Buddha who was on his round in the city, and asked him why he did that thing which caused a great shame and disdain to his father and to all the royal families. That was because King Suddhodana still thought and saw the Buddha as his son who was born in his monarchy family, so he should not behave himself as a beggar. To the king's question the Buddha in his standing posture with his alms-bowl in both hands replied, "Oh, Great King! I am no longer a prince, nor do I belong to the monarchy caste any longer. I did give up the monarchy system and left behind the kingdom, the parents, the wife, and the son, and then became a monk in search for Buddhahood to liberate all beings from suffering and to realize nirvana. I am a Buddha. You are a King. In the Buddhas' tradition we live on collecting alms-food once a day from those donors who give their things freely and benevolently. I simply follow such a tradition, which is not yours, and has nothing to do with you, your tradition, and your royal families. Please understand this fact and the issue you have in mind."

Having heard the Buddha's wise and honest words his father, King of Kapilavatthu, found his mind open and his heart awakened, and therefore he accepted with no reserve those words uttered eloquently by the Master of the world. He then surrendered himself to the Buddha and extended his invitation to the Buddha and his twenty thousand monks to his Royal Palace for breakfast. At the end of breakfast the Buddha delivered a dharma talk based on *ariyavamsika-sutta*[18] to his father, his royal families, and the dignitaries present at the gathering in the immense chamber. Listening attentively and mindfully, King Suddhodana reached an initial enlightenment and entered the stream/flow of nirvana while all others benefited from his significant and meaningful discourse some right understanding, some right discernment, some right thought, and broad realization as well as definitive transformation in accordance with their personal, diverse developments in their varieties. In brief, everyone achieved peace of mind, universal love of heart, and elixir of waking up.

---

[18] The essence of the sutta, I believe, is about details of *Aryan clan* and *ariyadhamma*. The latter consists of factors pertaining to enlightenment (bhojjanga), mindfulness with regard to body, feeling, mind, and intellectual & spiritual subjects (satipatthâna); immeasurable freedom (vimutti); the ways and means to success, both worldly and spiritual (iddhipâda); insights (ñâna); and eightfold path or middle way (magga). Since the actual text could not be found, I rely on the meanings of "*ariya*" given in *Pali-English Dictionary* by Rhys Davids and Stede, published by Pali Text Society.

Mudra 31

Mudra 31

Mudra of Receiving A Mongo Fruit

In this mudra the Buddha was seated in the samadhi posture with his left hand opened and placed on his lap while his right hand rested on his right knee with the open palm holding a mongo which was clearly visible.

Illustrating Story:

After teaching and helping his father attain the first, the second, and the third levels of enlightenment, the Buddha remained in Kapilavatthu for three months observing Lent as all the Buddhist monks do. During that period of time he taught and assisted his stepmother, **Pajâpati Gotamî**, and his ex-wife, **Bimbâ** or **Yasodharâ** by name, to achieve the realization of nirvana, entering its eternal current technically called "*sotapanna*". In addition, he gave ehibhikkhu ordination to **Nanda**, his younger half-brother born of a different mother, and let Sariputta, his right hand disciple, ordain his son, Râhula, who then became the first novice in Buddhasâsana. He also taught a great many cousins and relatives up to the point that they established themselves in *ariyadhamma* (noble dharmas ranging from sotapanna – initial enlightenment, to arahatta - complete enlightenment). After the Lent and rainy season was over, he returned to Veluvana Monastery in Râjagaha City, the capital of Magadha State.

Some time later, a billionaire, Anâthapindika, who lived in Sâvatthi, came over to visit with the Buddha, and after attentively listening and hearing heedfully (with pure awareness or awareness without thought) the dharma expounded by the Great Master, became sotapanna (achiever of initial enlightenment). Then he made a generous offering to him and to his monks, and then extended his invitation to the Buddha to spend the Lent together with his noble monks in Sâvatthi. Upon his return to his city Anâthapindika bought a large and beautiful botanic garden from a young Prince, Jetu by name, with some millions of his money for building a monastery in which those monks headed by the Buddha could stay peacefully and comfortably. That monastery then earned the title name, "Jetavana Vihâra". There at Jetavana Vihâra, the Buddha spent a great deal of his time residing and teaching Dharma to countless number of those seeking his compassionate help in accomplishing enlightenment and realizing the ultimate truth of nirvana. King Pasenadi, Great King of Kosala, another Super Power State, was included in those seekers after truth. Like the Great King of Magadha State, Bimbisara, he turned out to be another grand supporter of the Buddha and his Sâsana.

At that time there was a millionaire of Râjagaha City who apparently had no religious profession. Nonetheless, he was interested in finding out what religion to follow or adhere to. During such a moment of contemplation a great idea occurred in him that he should have the sandalwood in his possession to be made into an alms-bowl and to have it hoisted on the utmost top of a very tall bamboo tree in front of his house. To materialize such an idea he hired the best carpenter in town to make it to his satisfaction. Then, he had that sandalwood bowl hung on the very top of his bamboo tree. After that he announced publicly that whoever became an arahatta (perfectly enlightened person) should fly up in the sky to pick that special bowl and bring it down to him. Such was a way to prove to him that there existed an arahatta, as many spiritual masters of various doctrines and belief systems claimed to be.

A few days later many disciples, one after another, of diverse doctrines and disciplines came over to visit with him and told him all wonderful and miraculous things about their masters. But the millionaire insisted that if any of them was genuinely an arahatta should demonstrate their supernatural powers by flying over the sky and pick the designated bowl himself so that he would pay respect to him and accept him as his master or spiritual mentor. When seven-day dateline for proving if there existed an arahatta nearly came to an end, still no master of any kind dared to show him any miracle and magic power (because perhaps none had ever had it as claimed).

When the millionaire was just about to make a public announcement that there was no arahatta in the world, two great disciples of the Buddha, Mahamoggallana and Pindola Bhâradavâja were out of the monastery and at one point stood calmly and in serene quietude on a huge flat rock. They happened to hear some passing-by people talking about a millionaire's announcement to which no master of any religion showed up to demonstrate his supernatural power, and that the millionaire of Râjagaha city would announce publicly that there existed no arahatta in the world. Then, Mahamoggallana asked Pindola if he had heard what those people talked about, and Pindola responded positively. They both thought in a similar way that the millionaire and many people were about to cause some harm to religion, so Mahamoggallana suggested to Pindola that he demonstrate his supernatural power by flying through the sky and picking up that sandalwood alms-bowl. In response to Mahamoggallana's suggestion, Pindola said that Mahamoggallana possessed such a power much more than he does, and therefore Mahamoggallana should carry out the demonstration. Realizing that Mahamoggallana would not do it, Pindola then entered in the fourth jhânic, meditative absorption, which is the base of special knowledge and full emancipation as well as psychic powers or abhiññâ [19], demonstrating his supernatural power by grabbing a three-foot long flat rock with

---

[19] The list of abhiññâ is: Levitation, heavenly ear (clairaudience), knowing others' thoughts (thought-reading), recollecting one`s previous lives, knowing other people`s rebirths, and certainty of emancipation already attained (final assurance).

his toes and flying in the sky as if the rock were simply a cotton flake hanging on those toes of his. He then circulated round and round above Râjagaha city seven times, making himself appear like a large pot's lid to cover that city.

The Râjagaha citizens were absolutely startled and utterly horrified that the flat rock would fall on their heads and requested that Pindola hold it firmly in his toes. But he instead let it get blown back and forth, and then fell down on the place wherefrom it was picked up, and he then stood in the sky in front of the millionaire's house. With the sight of such an immense psychic power demonstration, the millionaire surrendered and paid his respect to Venerable Pindola asking him to come in and take a seat in his house while he arranged for the sandalwood alms-bowl to be brought down and offered it to the Elder Pindola who, after receiving it, flew back to the monastery just like a bird returning home with its rapid flight.

Upon hearing such a demonstration by Pindola Bhâradavâja the Buddha immediately laid down a monastic rule prohibiting his disciples from showing any supernatural power in public. Also, he gave his order to destroy the sandalwood alms-bowl by breaking it up into small pieces and making each piece a kind of medicinal remedy.

Having learned of the Buddha's new rule regarding the supernatural power demonstration, those heretics became extremely happy, and then made their plans of carrying out such a demonstration dispatching their followers to announce everywhere that their masters would demonstrate their supernatural powers in competition with Monk Gotama.

King Bimbisara, after being briefed on the matter concerned by his press secretary and national security adviser, approached the Buddha at the monastery and asked him about his rule of prohibiting his monks from demonstrating their supernatural powers in public. Responding to his hot question the Buddha said, "Yes, Great King!" The king further inquired about what he would do if those heretics, the rivals of his, would demonstrate their powers, to which the Great Master of the world declared he would do it himself. To another important question regarding the said rule put to him by King Bimbisara the Buddha disclosed that, although he laid down the rule, but it was only for his monks to observe, he as the Chief and Master was not bound by such a rule made up by himself. He further compared himself to an owner of a mango grove who prohibited all others from picking any mongo of his, but not him who owned the grove himself. Then, the Buddha told King Bimbisara that he would show his supernatural power in Sâvatthî city on full moon day of âsâlha (around October) about four months from then on.

On part of the heretics, after mocking on the Buddha accusing him of escaping confrontation with them by departing from Râjagaha for Sâvatthî, had a large structure of building constructed and decorated beautifully and neatly and announced that they would demonstrate their supernatural powers right there. Hearing such a rumor, King Pasenadi, the Buddha's great supporter, approached the Master to inquire if what he heard was true, and after receiving his confirmation offered to build an immense vihâra for him to show his supernatural power to subdue his rivals. The Buddha refused to accept the king's offer since it was not necessary, and then told him that he would do such a demonstration under a mango tree.

Upon knowing of the Buddha's plan those heretics hired a great many people to cut down all mango trees grown in public places so as to prevent him from carrying out his plan since they were extremely afraid of his supreme power.

When the full moon day of October was drawing near, that early morning of the full moon day the Buddha together with hundreds of his monks entered Sâvatthî city for collecting alms-food. He encountered a royal gardener, Gantha by name, carrying in his hand a ripe mango fruit, which he picked from the king's garden. On glancing at the Buddha and his grace the gardener was so exceedingly enthused and deeply moved that he offered to him that delicious mango which he intended to bring to King Pasenadi.

After receiving that special mango from Gantha, the Buddha indicated to Ananda, his attendant monk, that he wanted to sit down. Ananda then prepared the seat for him, and then he sat down and straightaway handed the mango over to Ananda so that he could make a juice for him to drink. After drinking it, he handed the mango's seed to Gantha instructing him to dig a hole and plant it in the soil, which he did as instructed. The Buddha washed his hand of that mango's seed, and then, all of a sudden, those present witnessed a miracle, that is to say, the mango's seed grew up instantaneously and for some brief moments Gantha together with the monks present at the gathering were observing the event with their astonishment the little mango tree was gradually growing, growing, and growing and eventually producing five large branches. Each branch extended in space about fifty feet in length, and at the same time blossomed and bore abundant, countless fruits both raw and ripe all over the mango tree. Meanwhile some of them fell down to earth and became available for anyone to pick and eat freely and, of course, deliciously. That brought to Gantha so tremendous joy and indescribable happiness that he enthusiastically picked those fallen mangos and offered them to those monks who accompanied the Buddha so that they could eat them with appreciation and mindfulness.

Mudra 32

Mudra 32

Mudra of Performing Twin Miracles

In this mudra the Buddha was seated on a throne (special high seat) with both feet placed on a lotus-flower (like sitting on a chair) while his left hand rested on his upper left thigh and his right hand was raised to his chest level with its palm slightly bent forward over the thumb, indicating the manner of elucidating dharma.

Illustrating Story:

After the Buddha got the mango tree known as "Gandamba" as he wished to have, he then was determined to perform a twin miracle, the miracle of the double appearances, to refute the heretical masters. In the afternoon of full moon day of âsâlha month, the day on which Ganda planted the mango seed at his instruction. He then emerged from his gandha-kuti (lodging cottage filled with delightful smells of incense and scented ointment or perfume) and stood with a graceful dignity in the frontal hall in the midst of his monks, nuns, and lay devotees who assembled there for the sole purpose of admiring and witnessing the Master's miracle performance. At the initial stage, the Buddha invented miraculously a large crystal platform installed on such widely expanding gandamba tree decorated naturally with all its beauty and wonder, and then went up through his elevating power and seated himself on such an utmost outstanding crystal platform and performed the twin miracle as follows:

1. *A pipe of glowing fire burst out of the upper part of his body while a water current of flowed out forcefully from the lower part of his body. Then, in reverse, the fire pipe rushed out of the lower part of his body while*

the swift water current ran speedily through the upper part of his body.
2. The glowing fire pipe steamed out of his body front part while from the back part the torrent of waters speeded its fast flow. Such a phenomenon then repeated itself in reverse order.
3. The glowing fire pipe rushed out from his right eye while from his left eye hurriedly ran out the water current. Here, once again, such a phenomenon repeated itself in reverse order.
4. The glowing fire pipe erupted through his right ear while through his left ear hastened swiftly the water current. Once again, the reverse order of such a phenomenon was repeated.
5. The glowing fire pipe rushed out through his right nose while through his left nose burst out speedily the water current. This was then repeated in the reverse order.
6. The glowing fire pipe rushed out through his right arm while through his left arm burst out swiftly the water current. This was then repeated in the reverse order.
7. The glowing fire pipe rushed out from his right hand while from his left hand burst out hurriedly the water current. This was then repeated in the reverse order.
8. The glowing fire pipe rushed out through his physical right torso while through his physical left torso ran out swiftly the water current. This was then repeated in the reverse order.
9. The glowing fire pipe rushed out from his right fingers while from his left fingers burst out the water current. This was then repeated in the reverse order.
10. The glowing fire pipe rushed out from a piece of hair while the water current burst out from another piece of hair. Such a phenomenon went on and on in pairs as previously described throughout his physical body. When such a glowing fire rushed out, it manifested

alternately in six colors, namely, green, yellow, red, white, blue, and violet.

When a color shined forth from the fire and reflected on the water, and then caused the water to change its color into the same color as that of fire. This went on and on alternately, which created a great wonder beyond an adequate description. The farther the fire pipe and water current rushed forth, the brighter and more vastly lit the sky became. In this way, millions of people all over Sâvatthî and its neighboring towns and villages could see vividly and with amazement and bewilderment.

Finally, the Buddha invented another Buddha totally identical with him and let the invented Buddha mirror his movement and activity as the real Buddha was manifesting. For example, when the Buddha performed his mindful walking, the invented Buddha would do the same, or when he seated himself in his samadhi posture, the invented Buddha would do that as well. In case of the Buddha posing a question, the invented Buddha would reply; and when the invented Buddha asked a question, the real Buddha would answer him, and so on and so forth.

At the end of the twin miracle performance, the Buddha delivered a distinguished discourse appropriate to the occasion, and a great many people, who witnessed such a performance of his, attained to the highest knowledge (*pure awareness*) and achieved realization of truth as well as got radically transformed. They were all greatly joyful and immeasurably blissful (*attamanâ*).

Mudra 33

Mudra 33

Mudra of Teaching and Helping His Mother

In this mudra the Buddha was seated in the samadhi posture with his left hand placed on the sole of his left foot while his right hand was raised to the chest level with its fingers slightly bent forward and the thumb bent toward and almost touching those fingers. Such a mudra indicates his manner of expounding the dharma. In another representation, the fingers were positioned suggesting a way of summoning someone, which was in accordance with the story of asking his mother to get closer to him for listening attentively to that dharma which he wished to impart to her.

Illustrating Story:

During the moments of performing the twin miracle, an inner inquiry occurred in him that all the Buddhas in the past had gone somewhere after their performances of the twin miracles. Then, he instantaneously knew through his insight that they all ascended to Távatimsa heaven for spending Lent (a three-month period of contemplation) and rescued and liberated their mothers from the cycle of birth-death-samsaric life. Therefore, he would follow their example, and he actually did go up to that heaven over which Indra reigned. In that ascension, the Buddha lifted his right foot from the crystal platform (used for his twin-miracle performance) and placed it on the topmost summit of *Yugandhara* mountain, while his left foot was moved upward and placed on the very top of *Sineru* mountain; then seated himself on the throne called "Pandukambala[20]" set up by Indra and his fellow devas.

---

[20] Pandu literally means pale-red or yellow (reddish, light yellow, grey) while kambala refers to a light red blanket or yellow-colored cloth. When combined together "Pandukambala" is a pale-red, orange-colored cloth for

At the time of his disappearing from the human world those people who came to witness and observe his twin-miracle performance were wondering where he had gone: to Cittagûta mountain or to Krailas mountain? Since none of them knew for certain, they were all waiting for his return since the disappearance of the Buddha was for them as if the light beam had been turned off from the planet Earth. Meanwhile, some people approached the Venerable Mahamoggallana who specialized in supernatural, psychic powers, and he told them to ask the Venerable Anuruddha, who then informed them of the Buddha's taking his residence in tâvatimsa heaven for the purpose of teaching *abhidharma* to his mother. To their question about the length of time for his residence in that heaven Anuruddha Thera said to them, "three months," and asked them to remain where they were or return to Sâvatthî for welcoming the Buddha back at the end of the Lent Observation.

The majority of people decided to stay on and waited for the Buddha's returning to earth while Mahamoggallana Thera rendered his services of delivering dharma talks and answered their questions on a regular basis. Meanwhile the compassionate and benevolent millionaire, *Anâthapindika* by name, helped them in all possible ways so that they all could be comfortable and feel at ease.

Upon seeing the Buddha seated on his Pandukambala throne, *Sakka,* also known as *Indra,* King of tâvatimsa heaven, was extremely pleased and exceedingly delighted. So, he announced such a special, unprecedented event to all his devas (this heaven is known as tâvatimsa, which means thirty three, is traditionally taken to consist of thirty-three devas) and to many others devas from other heavens. As a result, a countless

---

covering Sakka's throne built on an ornamental stone. It's said that when King Sakka or Indra sat on it, the throne sank to a very comfortable position while on getting up it sprang up to stay at its normal position.

number of them came over to pay their respects to the Master of the human world, the world of devas, and the brahma world.

Looking around at such a massive, large crowd, the Buddha did not see his mother present there, so he then asked King Sakka if he saw his mother at all, to which he replied in a negative form. Nonetheless, he (King Sakka) asked for the Buddha's permission to go up to dusita heaven to have an audience with devaditâ Siri Mahamâyâ, the Buddha's mother. So, he went up there straightaway, and invited her to come down to his heaven, tâvatimsa, so that she could see her son, the Buddha, who would impart to her an appropriate dharma. The Buddha's mother then took leave of her dusita heaven and descended with grace to tâvatimsa heaven where her son, the Buddha, was staying and awaiting her arrival. After exchanging the proper greetings, she took a seat on a beautifully decorated place set up for her amidst those devas and devaditâs from all the six heavens. Then, the Buddha gently and gratefully pulled his right hand out of his robe and said to her tenderly: *ehi amma*, which means *welcome mother*!! He then expounded coherently and thoroughly *abhidharma* (his higher teachings on practical philosophy and depth psychology) for a period of three months. In Eastern culture, such an action taken by the Buddha was said to be repaying for milk that his mother had nurtured and nourished him when he was a baby. At the end of his three-month teaching and expounding of abhidharma (twelve volumes in written Pali text), Devaditâ Siri Mahamâyâ attained to the Noble Path and Noble Fruition (Enlightenment).

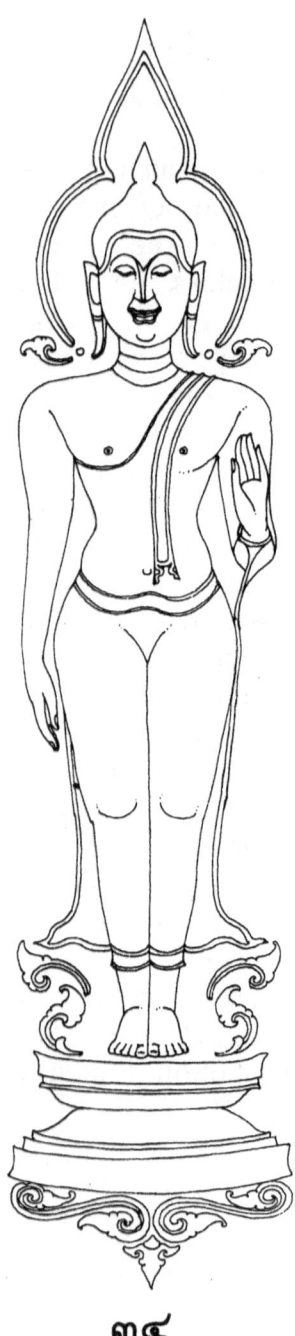

Mudra 34

Mudra 34

Mudra of Prohibiting the Core of Sandalwood

In this mudra the Buddha was in his standing posture with his right hand hanging down along side of his body while his open left hand rose to his chest level, with the palm facing forward, away from his body. Such a signal indicates the act of prohibition.

Illustrating Story:

The following story does not exist in Pali literature of Theravada Buddhism. It's told from generation to generation and therefore, it could have been an oldest chronicle regarding the Buddha images (Buddha-rûpa), that is to say, it could be the first Buddha image constructed in his time when he stilled lived. It's quite bizarre that Theravada Buddhists do not reject the existence of such a Buddha image made of special sandalwood but accept it as an accepted basis for study. Therefore, this mudra of prohibiting the core of sandalwood appears to be an ancient account worthy to be included as one of the Buddha's various recognized mudras.

The story which we can relate was as follows: After the Buddha had ascended to tâvatimsa heaven for the sole purpose of teaching and helping his mother in the heavenly plane of life, King Pasenadi missed him so much so that he was thinking of having the most excellent sandalwoodthat ever existed in his kingdom made into an image of the Buddha. So, he commanded the great artists and carpenters to search for such a block of sandalwood, and to carve a Buddha image with it. When the work was done, he had the sandalwood Buddha image installed in the chamber where the Buddha used to sit when he came to the royal grand palace for a visit with him or for performing a ceremony so that the Buddha would then be able to behold the image at any time.

Then, after the Buddha descended to Earth from tâvatimsa heaven, the Great King of Kosala State invited him and his monks one day to the palace to have a meal. Then and there he asked his aide to bring the sandalwood Buddha image down from the shrine to show to the Buddha. Upon glancing at the image the Buddha raised his left hand in the gesture of prohibition and simultaneously uttered thus: *evam nisîdatha*, meaning, please remain in such a seat as you have been. Through such an utterance of the Buddha the sandalwood Buddha moved back to the shrine where he was inaugurated. At that particular moment, King Pasenadi felt a great wonder and astonishment witnessing such an amazing event that took place in front of him surrounded by his royal cousins and dignitaries. He then offered with high respect and reverence to the Buddha and those monks accompanying him the well-prepared breakfast food, which consisted of various nourishing, healthful, and full-strength ingredients.

At the end of breakfast, the Buddha Jinasiha[21] delivered a distinguished discourse and took leave together with his monk disciples for Jetavana Monastery.

---

[21] Another title of the Buddha, meaning Great Victorious One, just like a lion, King of forest.

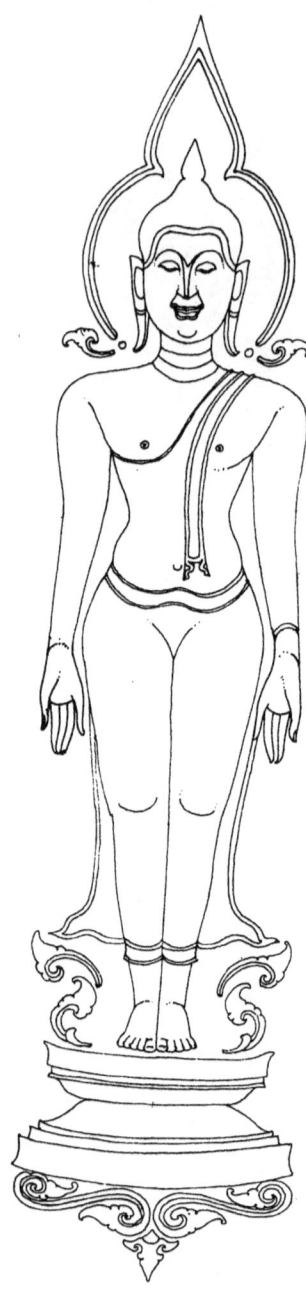

๓๕

Mudra 35

Mudra 35

Mudra of Opening the World

In this mudra the Buddha was in his standing posture with both hands stretching down alongside his body and the palms of his hands opened and pointed toward the front, away from his body. This indicates the gesture of opening up something.

Illustrating Story: Details of the story are included in the mudra number 37, the ***Mudra of Descending from Tâvatimsa Heaven***. Please read it all there.

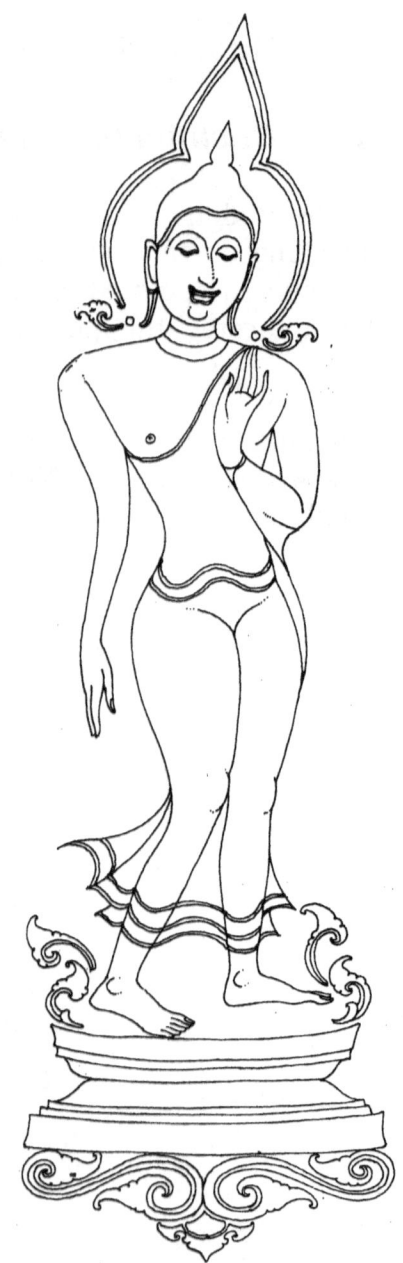

Mudra 36

Mudra 36

Mudra of Graceful Walking/Dallying

In this mudra the Buddha was in his standing posture, elevating his right heel off of the ground while his toes still touched it firmly, which indicates a preparation for taking a step. His right hand stretched downward in a manner of swinging, while his left hand was upstretched to his chest level with its open palm extended forward, indicating the style of graceful walking or mindful dallying.

Illustrating Story:

As a matter of fact, the act of walking mindfully and dallying gracefully is the Buddha's regular, normal practice, which doesn't seem to be so significant that the Buddha image of this mudra would be built. Nonetheless, at the time of his descending from tâvatimsa heaven accompanied by devas and brahmas, the procession was filled with enormous wonder and seen to be beautiful beyond an adequate description that Venerable Sariputta (the Buddha's Right Hand Disciple) became so greatly joyful and tremendously enthusiastic that he uttered the following verse:

> *Such most gorgeous and picturesque grace of the Great Master I have never seen before, nor have I ever heard of any admiring voice spoken by anyone regarding such glorious beauty of his physical body. So, the Buddha gifted with paramount loving and caring voice descends to Earth from Dusita[22] Heaven.[23]*

---

[22] Another heaven higher up from Tâvatimsa. The Buddha's mother was said to be living there, in Dusita Heaven, before, at the time of, and after his visit with her.
[23] In Pali: na me dittho ito buppe na suto uda kassaci evam vaggugado satthâ dusita ganimâgato.

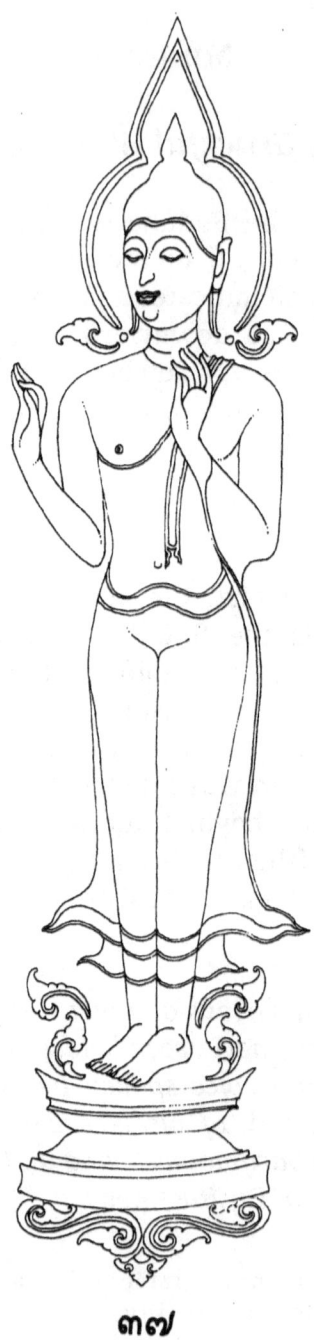

Mudra 37

Mudra 37

Mudra of Descending from Tâvatimsa

In this mudra the Buddha was in his standing posture with both hands raised to his chest level similar to the mudra of stopping his relatives from waging war. The only difference lies in the fact that the joint fingers of both hands of his formed into the gesture of teaching the dharma.

Illustrating Story:

Details of this story cover the mudras no. 35 and no. 36 as well. Here is the complete story: After the Buddha ascended to tâvatimsa heaven for teaching abhidharma to his mother and for spending Lent (a period of three months' contemplation during the Indian rainy season), the mass of countless people, upon receiving the reliable news of his descending to Earth from Mahamoggallana Thera, prepared themselves traveling and setting up tents around Samkassa city where he would go down so that they could behold him with their own eyes. So, at the end of his three-month stay in tâvatimsa heaven, which was the very day following full moon day of November, all kinds of people from various places together with monks and nuns headed by Venerable Sariputta assembled enthusiastically inside, outside, and all around Samkassa Nagara (city) awaiting his arrival patiently.

When the full moon day of assayuja-mâsa arrived, the Buddha summoned to his residence King Sakka and told him about his intention to descend to the planet Earth, the human world. Upon knowing of his definite plan Sakka, King of Tâvatimsa Heaven, invented through his enormous psychic powers three ladders, namely, a gem ladder in the middle, a gold ladder on the right, and a silver ladder on the left, and all of them setting their feet on earth just outside the principal gate of

Samkassa Nagara while their heads or top parts fixed at the topmost summit of the mount Sineru. The Buddha then descended on the gem ladder, whilst the accompanying devas and brahmas went down along the gold ladder and the silver ladder, respectively. It was said that devas and brahmas all over ten thousand universes gathered together to see the Buddha off, which was the most spectacular, breathtaking scene of gathering that ever occurred in the heavenly plane of existence.

At the appropriate moment in time, the Buddha stood on the head of his ladder surrounded by numerous devas and brahmas, and performed a *miracle of opening the worlds*, technically known as "*lokavivarana*" by glancing with his eyes in ten directions, including above and below. Through the Buddha's supreme power, everywhere it became instantaneously transparent with no impediment whatsoever, and therefore all heavenly celestials could behold all human beings and vice versa; and all beings in hell, in yama[24] world, and in every planet could see one another for the first time. In addition, through such a miracle performance, the Buddha radiated simultaneously from him six glowing and gleaming colors of white, red, blue, black, grey, and violet, which was utterly a great wonder and an amazement.

The Buddha then started descending along the gem ladder escorted by King Sakka together with all the devas on the gold ladder and Brahma Sahampati accompanied by all the brahmas on the silver ladder. In his front, Pañcasikhara Gandabba Deva played an orange-colored violin and sang a beautiful song with his matchless, wonderful voice, on both sides of his gem ladder Sandusita Deva and Suyâma Deva offered

---

[24] World of the dead, and its ruler is called, "Yama," who is actually King of the dead (ghosts or peta-hungry ghosts included).

him their special divine cloths called "camara[25]" while Pajâpati Brahma held the majestic umbrella above his head, and King Indra Deva carried the Buddha's alms-bowl by name of "selamaya[26]" and guided him on the way down to the planet Earth.

As soon as the Buddha set his feet on the ground those massive spectators beheld his most magnificently charming body and watched with their stunning eyes his graceful and mindful walking amidst the numerous devas and brahmas as Sariputta already resonated previously (to repeat):

> *Such most gorgeous and picturesque grace of the Great Master I have never seen before, nor have I ever heard of any admiring voice spoken by anyone regarding such glorious beauty of his physical body. So, the Buddha gifted with paramount loving and caring voice descends to Earth from Dusita[27] Heaven.*[28]

Finally, the great compassionate Buddha delivered a distinguished dharma lecture to his largest and all-integrated congregation. And at the end of his unsurpassed discourse, thousands and thousands of humans, devas, and brahmas attained to realization of Dharma (Truth) and to irretrievable liberation from suffering.

---

[25] Literally, a yak (an animal of the cow family, that lives in central Asia) or a kind of antelope, so, that type of cloth would look like a bushy tail of a yak, or one kind of the royal ensigns.
[26] Made of Stone.
[27] Another heaven higher up from Tâvatimsa. The Buddha's mother was said to be living there, in Dusita Heaven, before, at the time of, and after his visit with her.
[28] In Pali: na me dittho ito buppe na suto uda kassaci evam vaggugado satthâ dusita ganimâgato.

Mudra 38

Mudra 38

Mudra of Full Lotus-Sitting Posture (Diamond-Samadhi Posture)

In this mudra the Buddha was seated in a particular sitting posture, that is, in the full lotus-position, with both soles of his feet raised and placed on his lap while his two hands were placed on top of each other and rested on his two soles. This way of sitting is traditionally known as "diamond-samadhi posture".

Illustrating Story:

There is no reference text that describes details of this mudra, but it is believed that it's a resting posture during the daytime. As a matter of fact, this manner of sitting is not very comfortable; so to say that it's a resting position is not quite correct. On the contrary, his manner of holding himself in such a position implies an act of doing something, in place of resting and taking it easy. Nonetheless, there is no descriptive text on the matter concerned. So, it's beyond the capacity of the author to make up a story, and therefore let the issue be a research work for those interested in this mudra. Certainly, it is rare to find the Buddha image with the diamond-samadhi posture, since it's not popular among the Buddhists.

Maybe, the Buddha was practicing a hatha yoga posture!!

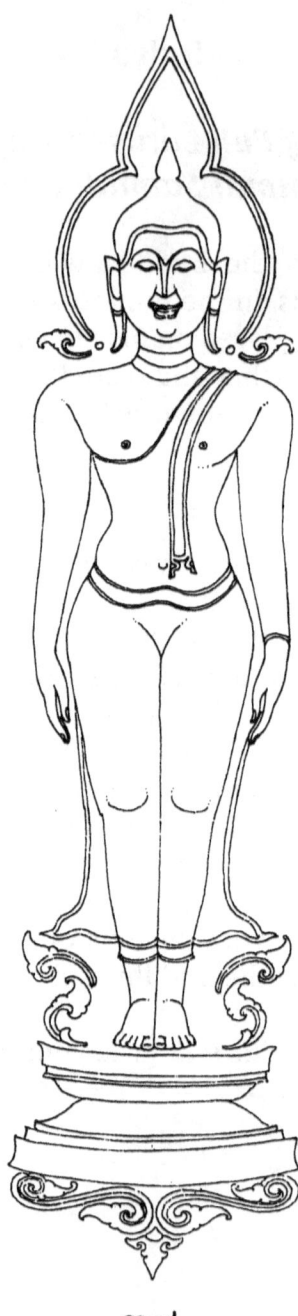

Mudra 39

Mudra 39

Mudra of Standing

In this mudra the Buddha was in his normal standing posture with both hands stretching down comfortably along the side his body showing that there is no event taking place, which will cause him to move any part of his physical body. So, it is just a typical standing posture in which he conducts himself on a regular, standard basis.

Illustrating Story:

As a matter of fact, there is no text worth bringing up for describing this mudra in detail apart from stating that such a standing mudra is deeply registered in the memory of the Buddha's disciples. That is to say, every morning whether he would go out to a benevolent person's house following his invitation or emerge from his gandha-kuti for inspecting the readiness and orderliness of the monks, he would hold himself mindfully in such a usual standing posture. When his thorough inspection was over and all the monks present were well prepared for moving forward together, he would then lead them marching on.

Usually, before taking leave of his gandha-kuti for the reason of conducting his monks in their normal walk to some place (s), the attendant monk, Ananda, would brief the Buddha inside his residence informing him of the readiness and orderliness of the monks, and of the right moment for leaving and going somewhere. Even so, he would mindfully and gracefully come out of his gandha-kuti, and would stand in the front balcony and inspect his monks thoroughly before leading them and marching on without any hurry.

Such a behaving function of the Buddha indicates his heart and mind filled with mettâ (universal, unconditional, and illimitable love), and karunâ (compassion and empathy) for his monks and nuns. In addition, such a conduct carried out by the Great Master should be a norm (model) for all the chief monks in the Monastic Community.

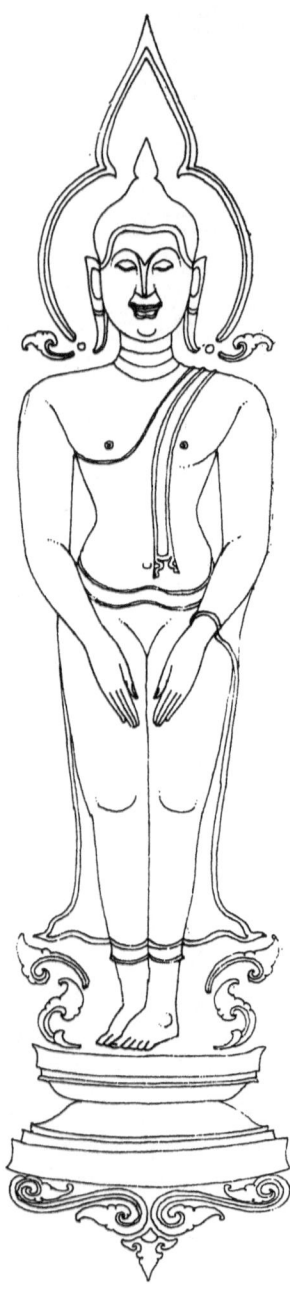

Mudra 40

Mudra 40

Mudra of Establishing His Footprint

In this mudra the Buddha was in his standing posture with his left foot stepping on his right foot, indicating the act of pressing and imprinting the foot, with both hands intertwined and rested on his thighs with a perfect restraint. Such an act implies the Buddha's intention to establish his footprint with all the complete aspects of the foot intact so that it could remain visible for a long time.

Illustrating Story:

At one time the Buddha took his residence at the Ghositârâma Monastery situated in Kosambî city and delivered many discourses to those seeking his help and guidance. It was reported that a great many people took refuge in the Buddha, Dharma, and Sangha, and also attained to Noble Path and Noble Fruition (the realization of truth and the achievement of enlightenment).

At that time in Kuru State there lived a brahman, "Mâgandiya" by name, possessed of abundant wealth and numerous properties, and had a wife called "Mâgandiyâ". They both had an extremely pretty daughter who was absolutely dear to them beyond words, and who bore the same name as her mother. The father, Mâgandiya Brahman, was awfully cautious about choosing a husband for his daughter because of her unmatched beauty and of his plentiful wealth and richness. Therefore, he found it utterly difficult to give his daughter to any man who would ask to marry her since he always thought that such a man did not deserve to be her husband.

One day at dawn the Buddha was surveying the world through his specific meditation, that was, by means of his *awakened eye*, the Eye of Insight. He then perceived Mâgamdiya's and his wife's high capacities and ripe faculties for achieving the Noble Path and Noble Fruition. So, right away, he picked his alms-bowl and put on his monk's robe and set out his trip alone heading toward the fire worship shrine located just outside of his house.

That early morning Brahman Mâgandiya left for his fire worship shrine in order to perform his worshipping ceremony as he did routinely. All of a sudden, he had a glance of the Buddha who possessed the most beautiful body with all its radiant faculties, which he had never seen before. Then he thought the man in his sight would be appropriate for his daughter, so he returned home with haste to tell his wife about the most handsome man on earth. Upon hearing her husband describing excitingly and admiring the man with all his heart and mind, she responded positively that they go back to meet with the man, following her husband's suggestion.

Arriving at the sight where he saw him, unfortunately the Buddha was not there but had hid himself in a place nearby. What he left in the previous place was his footprint, which Mâgandiya's wife examined thoroughly since she had studied the text on reading human footprints and was well versed in discerning them correctly. After reading and contemplating on the Buddha's footprint, she then told her husband that such an incredible footprint did not belong to an ordinary person, but was of someone excellent and most exalted in the world. She further explained to him the characteristics of human footprints thus:

> *A footprint of the person obsessed by lustful desire has a large hole in the middle of the sole without touching the ground.*

For the person dictated by hate, his footprint presses the heel hard on the ground.

The footprint of the person conquered by delusion, confusion, self-deception, and bewilderment has its toes dipping into the ground.

But a person who has such an even sole (with all its parts touching the ground completely) as that man has, is an extraordinary man who has no râga (lust), dosa (hate), and moha (delusion).

In the midst of their conversations the Buddha emerged from his hiding place and appeared in front of them. With the sight of the Buddha, Brahman Mâgandiya pointed toward him telling his wife that he was the man who left his footprint on the ground, and the man whom he had previously seen. The husband was attempting to talk his wife into accepting the man (the Buddha) and inviting him to their house for the purpose of persuading him to marry their daughter. The Buddha remained silent and immobile, only listening to them attentively and with compassion.

After a short while, he told them his brief personal history beginning from the time of renouncing the world and becoming a monk in search for perfect enlightenment and Buddhahood. Once his ultimate goal was accomplished, he started his Dharma Mission helping all beings liberate themselves from suffering and from the cycle of birth-death-samsaric life. At one point he related to them that on the full moon night of May before reaching enlightenment he was exceptionally tempted by three most beautiful young women, but by firmly holding on to his goal and unwaveringly sticking to the right knowledge (particular understanding and experience), he was not moved by such a temptation. Certainly, those three young women were ten times more beautiful than your daughter, the Buddha added, whom I would not dare to touch.

Finally, the Buddha delivered a distinguished discourse on the dharma appropriate to their character and development, and at the end of his sermon both Brahman Mâgandiya and his wife became irreversibly enlightened and therefore, resorted to the Three Gems, namely, Buddha, Dharma, and Sangha. He then asked for an ordination to join in with the Buddha's Order of Monks while his wife became a bhikkhuni (female monk). They gave their daughter to his young brother to look after together with all his fortune.

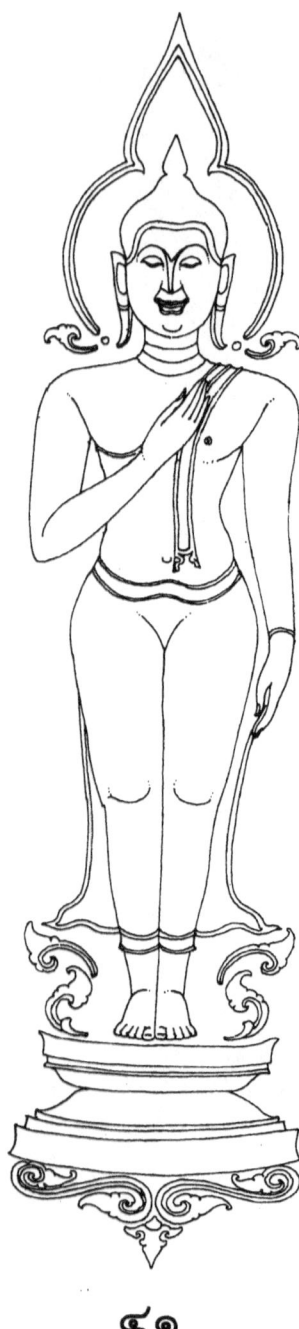

Mudra 41

Mudra 41

Mudra of Bathing in Rain Water

In this mudra the Buddha was in his standing posture dressing himself by covering one shoulder with a rain shower clothe (bathing garment) called vassikasâtaka while leaving the other shoulder open; his left hand was stretching down along side his body and his right hand was raised to the level of the upper chest. This indicates the act of bathing himself in the rainwater. Such a Buddha image is the same as the one of inviting rain to pour down on the earth.

Illustrating Story:

This Buddha's mudra was popularly built as an invitation extended to rain for coming down to nourish soil, plants, and trees since there was a grave drought in the Sâvatthî area. At that time the Buddha was staying at Jetavana Monastery, just outside of Sâvatthî city. The peasants and all kinds of agriculture workers suffered a critical drought that prevailed and spread out all over Kosala State, starting from its capital city, Sâvatthî. One day those professing Buddhasâsana thought of the Buddha and his supreme power and became totally convinced that he could do something to eliminate the drought and provide for their land and crops. So, they all approached him at his monastery, humbly and respectfully seeking his help so that their troubles caused by such a drought would be over. Their request was very simple, that is to say, the Buddha should take a shower in an opening space, even though at that time there was no sign of falling rain. After accepting their innocent request, the Buddha changed his robe to a bathing garment technically known as vassikasâtaka (shower clothe/cloak), and then went out to stand in the opening space, glancing his eyes all around mindfully and intently to all directions. After a short, while a magic rain started to pour down softly at first, and gradually got heavier and heavier through his unsurpassed psychic power. While they saw his capability to bathe himself in the rainwater, the massive crowd of Sâvatthî citizens and throughout Kosala State enjoyed their shower and bath beyond an adequate description.

Mudra 42

Mudra 42

Mudra of Rain Making[29]

In one version of this mudra, the Buddha was in his standing posture dressing in a bathing garment (udakasâtaka), raising his right hand in the manner of summoning someone, while his left hand has its open palm and is lifted up to the hip level. The gesture of both hands, even though in different manners, indicates the act of requesting rainfall.

Also the Buddha image of this mudra, as shown here, appeared in a sitting posture with his right hand formed in the same position as that of the Buddha image in the standing posture, but his left hand with its open palm rests on his lap. Such a posture likewise indicates the manner of asking for rainfall.

Some people prefer to call this mudra of rain making the "mudra of gandhâra" or "gandhâra rattha" for a simple reason that it was first erected in Gandhâra City around the year 400 Buddhist Era by King Milinda, the ruler of that city.

Illustrating Story:

At one time the Buddha took his residence at Jetavana Monastery situated in the outskirts of Sâvatthî. It happened that a grave drought reigned over the city and its vicinity up to the

---

[29] Whether true or false those two stories concerning the Buddha as a rainmaker are quite interesting since he brought on rain in both cases for the benefit of those people who suffered the droughts. Among Native Americans there are certain persons believed to have the power to make a rainfall. So, the completely self-developed person like the Buddha must have such power to make a rainfall, in addition to many psychic powers that he possesses.

point of lacking waters in ponds, in lakes, and in rivers, even in a huge pond of the Jetavana Monastery for monks' use was dried up.

One day after his return from his morning round of helping the people, the Buddha realized a serious difficulty and a great trouble that most people were going through. He was then strongly moved by compassion for both human beings and animals that suffered the drought, to do something for them all. First the Buddha ordered Ananda to get him some water for bathing, but he could not find it anywhere, so Ananda informed the Master of his empty-handed search for water. Then the Buddha told him what he meant for him to find was not the water in any place, but the rainwater. Hearing such a statement, Ananda became bewildered since there was no sign of rainfall at all. Nonetheless, out of his complete faith in the Master and his highest power, Ananda brought to him a rubbing cloth, and with a half of the cloth he covered the Buddha's physical body while the other half was placed on his shoulder hanging downward. After that the Buddha went to stand at the edge of the monastery's pond raising his right hand to call for rainfall and prepared his left hand for collecting rainwater. All of a sudden, numerous dark clouds were formed and then a heavy rain poured down on earth so that he himself could bathe in it, and as well, countless number of people all over Sâvatthî and throughout Kosala State were fortunate to take their baths and to enjoy abundant rainwater.

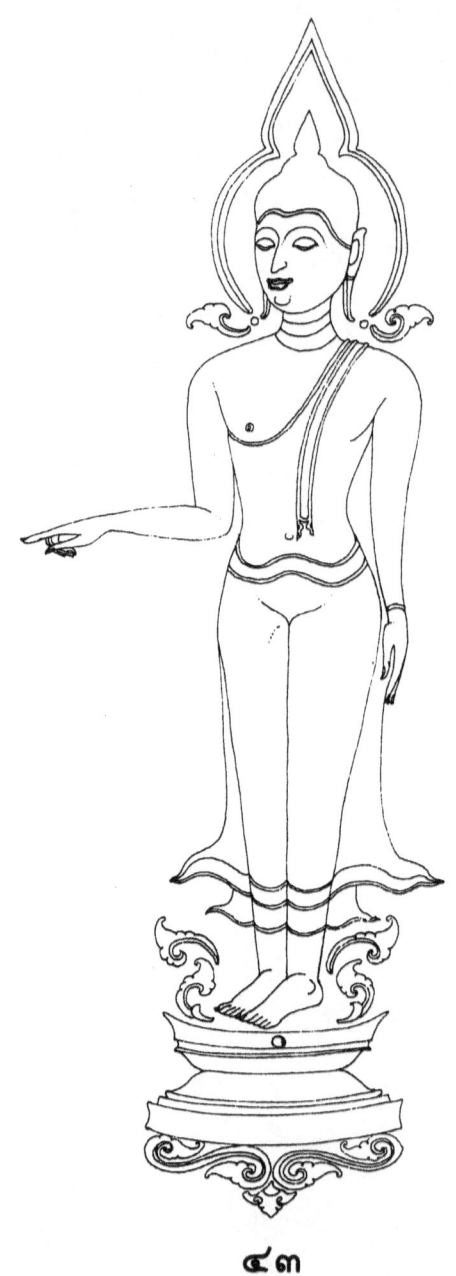

Mudra 43

Mudra 43

Mudra of Pointing to Loathsomeness

In this mudra the Buddha was in his standing posture with his left hand hanging down along side his body and his right hand raised to the waist level with his index finger pointing ahead, indicating an act of drawing attention to that which is loathsome.

Illustrating Story:

In the Buddha's epoch, in Râjagaha city there lived a beautiful prostitute who was quite an intelligent dancer and a fantastic singer to whom all men became especially infatuated because of her outstanding beauty and stunning voice. Her name was Sirima, and was the Doctor Jîvaka Komârabhacca's sister. Any man wanting to sleep with her was obliged to pay the equivalent of USD $4000 per night since she was a high class and most admirable prostitute of the epoch.

At that same time, living in the city of Râjagaha, there was also a female millionaire endowed with right understanding and perfect view, Uttarâ by name, a wife of Setthiputta, a billionaire, who was quite her opposite that is, he was a man of erroneous understanding and flawed view. She wished to have a short break from rendering her duty as his wife. Being a devout follower of the Buddha, she usually practiced free giving (dâna), observed certain moral precepts (sîla), and went to listen to his discourses at Veluvana Monastery. But after getting married to her husband and coming to live with him at his mansion, she did not have time for carrying out her normal practices, which made her very unhappy and extremely miserable. So, she dispatched a servant of hers to inform her father, millionaire Punna, of her troubles, and asked for a lump sum of money from him for spending on the meritorious deeds that she wanted to perform.

Upon receiving the satisfying amount of fund at her petition, she approached Sirima, the prostitute, requesting that she practice a wife's duty for her husband for a period of fifteen days during which she would pay her at her normal price and would provide for her all the requisites needed for comfort and worldly happiness so that she herself could do all the Buddhist practices as she used to.

When Sirima agreed to become a temporary wife for her husband, Uttarâ, wasting no time, went to have an audience with her Great Master, the Buddha, at his monastery, and informed him of all the arrangements that she had made in order to perform her Buddhist practices. Then, she invited the Buddha together with his monks to her house for having meals and delivering sermons on the dharma every single day for a period of fifteen days during which she would observe the precepts and offer food to him and his monks, no matter how many they were. After realizing that her Great Master had accepted her invitation, she went back home and prepared a variety of the healthy and delicious foods in her enormous kitchen with her own hands, assisted by her servants, of course. In so doing, she was extremely pleased and filled with great joy and immense enthusiasm.

Entering the fourteenth day, Uttarâ prepared a big feast since it was the last day of her meritorious performance. At a certain moment, Setthiputta, her husband, was standing near a window, looking out through a window and seeing his wife totally occupied with preparing and cooking various foods without taking care of her body so much but letting it sweat, with her clothes soaked with her sweat. He felt so funny inside himself that he exclaimed quietly thus, " Poor wife indeed! She did not like to be merely happy, and doing nothing much at home!! It's such a pity!!"

At that moment Sirima, the prostitute, was standing beside him, giving him a smile, and then left him alone. Then she thought about and pondered on a kind of romantic love and pleasures that she had been enjoying with him for a fortnight period, and by witnessing his unpleasant or even repulsive facial expression toward his wife, she further imagined that he definitely felt quite unhappy and dissatisfied with his wife who was so involved with a servant's job, instead of being a house mistress. Nonetheless, Sirima realized that she was hired to be just a temporary wife. Even so, she became suddenly envious, jealous, and hateful toward Uttarâ. She then went down to the kitchen, and there picked a laden from a stove, dipped it in hot cooking oil and poured it on Uttarâ's head and continued pouring it right down through her entire body.

Because of an astonishing power of mettâ and loving thought that she has for Sirima, Uttarâ did not feel any anger or even irritation toward her, let alone some burning sensations in her physical body. Instead she took it that Sirima was a commendable friend of hers since without her presence in the house for entertaining her husband, she wouldn't have been able to do her Buddhist obligation and responsibility as she had been doing for fourteen days. Although all her kitchen staff became terribly horrified by such an unexpected incident and went directly toward Sirima, pulling her hair and hitting her face really hard as well as pushing her down to the floor as an act of taking revenge for their mistress, Uttarâ then raised her hands and prohibited them to continue doing such a destructive thing once and for all saying thus: "Oh, my children! Stop, stop, stop, and get away!! Do not harm my helpful friend, Sirima." Immediately after that, she approached her (Sirima) and lifted her up from the kitchen floor, rubbing and touching her body lovingly as well as talking her into feeling at ease, free from fright, thus returning to her normal state of feeling and thinking.

Then, Sirima realized her position of being just an entertainer or entrepreneur, doing a highly paid job of entertaining Uttarâ's husband, and that she was not a house mistress as she imagined to be. She actually felt tremendously ashamed of her destructive behavior, especially when perceiving and witnessing Uttarâ's calmness, freedom from such negative feelings as anger, fury, and hate, and, instead, being kind, benevolent, and compassionate, Sirima felt a high respect and a double admiration for Uttarâ, she bent down toward her feet and prostrated to her in an Oriental manner of paying a great honor to a noble and respectful person.

Uttarâ then expressed her satisfaction and empathy to Sirima, telling her honestly how happy she was that she became mindful of her indecent and shocking behavior, and that in case of wishing to ask for forgiveness, she should do so with the Buddha, her Great Master. To her wise suggestion Sirima responded positively, even though she did not know of the Buddha at all. Uttarâ then told her that there would not be a problem since his heart was for all creatures that live on earth without discrimination, and that the following morning he would come to her house for breakfast together with his many monks. So Sirima was invited to be present at the gathering so that the Great Compassionate Master could help her fulfill whatever she wanted to. Upon hearing such beautiful and loving words from her, Sirima accepted Uttarâ's invitation and brought herself to participate in the breakfast offering in the hope that something wonderful would happen to her. After thanking Uttarâ with all her heart and mind, Sirima took leave and went upstairs to be with Setthiputta as she still had one more day to complete her contract.

The following morning the Buddha accompanied by his many monks came to Uttarâ's house for breakfast at her invitation. She then brought Sirima with her to pay proper respects to her highly revered Master and informed him of what had happened. At the same time she asked him to grant Sirima forgiveness as well as to give all those there a dharma talk as he used to.

Out of compassion for Sirima, the Buddha granted her full forgiveness and at the same time expressed his appreciation to Uttarâ for all her good deeds, particularly for the compassionate and noble behavior she showed to Sirima. In conclusion he uttered the following verses:

> *One should conquer one's own anger by neither getting angry at others nor at oneself (by love). One should overcome the evil in others through eradicating one's own evil. One should defeat one's own miserly or stinginess through benevolence and generosity. One ought to exterminate one's habitual behavior of speaking falsely and frivolously by true speech.*

At the end of his eloquent discourse Sirima together with all service women present at the gathering accomplished the initial but irreversible enlightenment and entered the eternal flow of nirvana.

After that Sirima invited the Buddha and his monks to her own house for breakfast in the following morning, which he accepted in serene silence. At the morning meal gathering presided by the Buddha, she requested that the receptionist monk at his monastery arrange for eight monks to come and receive food from her house everyday. She then asked to become an upâsikâ in Buddhasâsana, which was granted to her by the Buddha. Since then she gave up the prostitution practice throughout her life.

Toward the end of her life, Sirima got ill unexpectedly and eventually died of such a sudden illness: that particular morning she was fine and offered food to those eight monks as usual, but in the evening she just passed away peacefully.

To shorten the story, it was said that at the funeral ceremony the Buddha was present and pointed out to his monks and to all those people who came to pay their last respect to Sirima thus:

> *Behold and contemplate the dead body of Sirima that was pretty in its own nature and beautiful with dressing up and decoration, which was fully equipped with all required faculties and internal organs for the circulations of both accretion and excretion. The material body is entirely made up of conditioned things both material and mental, and is filled with attractive and loathsome constituents, which appears quite delightful to some but revolting to others depending on how they look at it. The body is certainly impermanent and constantly changing, and therefore in its existence it has no permanency or everlastingness. Eventually, all forms of the body end in death or total breaking up (disintegration), which is true to all living beings with no exception.*

At the end of his dharma preaching a great number of those present at Sirima's funeral realized the truth and attained to Noble Path and Noble Fruition.

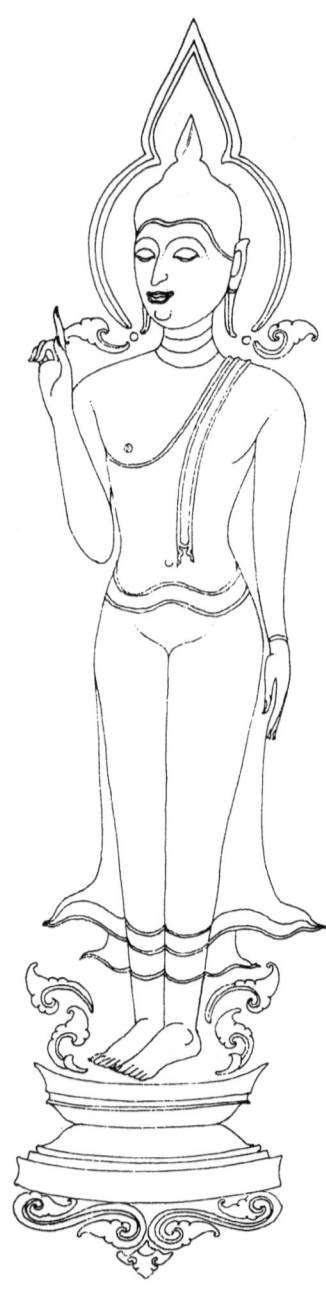

Mudra 44

Mudra 44

Mudra of Rebuking Mâra

In this mudra the Buddha was in his standing posture, with his left hand hanging down along side his body, and his right hand raised to the level of his face with the index finger pointing upward and forward, which implies "Rebuking Mâra".

Illustrating Story:

At one time the Buddha was staying at Veluvana Monastery near Râjagaha city, and during that time a monk, Kodhika by name, was practicing meditation diligently at *kâlasilâ* situated beside the mount *isigiri*. He put into his practice so a great effort and intelligence that *emancipation through mind* (mental freedom) resulting from temporary *attainment of fruition* was inevitable, meaning, he achieved it outright. Nonetheless, he failed to maintain such an achievement, so he fell off from it from time to time due to the fact that a severe chronicle sickness (incurable skin disease) impeded him to move forward toward a higher attainment. Although he could succeed in entering jhâna (meditative absorption) stage 1, stage 2, and stage 3 six times, then lost them when attempting to reach them a seventh time. One day before persevering to enter the jhânas, he thought to himself "I had already fallen off the jhánas six times. In fact, the fate of a meditator who failed so many times as I did, was not certain, in that he or she could go to a painful plane of life[30]". Peculiarly he brought a sharp razor to place beside him getting ready to cut his throat off during his meditation for the purpose of remaining in the jhânic meditation, and in turn making it a basis of Vipassana and moving onward rapidly to enlightenment. Then, Mâra knew of his thought and, to some extent, had some compassion for him

---

[30] In Pali: duggati.

since he (Mâra) perceived with some clarity a possibility of Kodhika's accomplishment of full enlightenment if he would take up the Vipassana Practice. Therefore, he decided to prohibit him from committing suicide, but realizing that Kodhika would not take him seriously, instead he approached the Buddha. He then disguised himself as a young man and went to have an audience with the Great Master of the world who was, of course, the monk Kodhika's master, and said to him the following stanza:

> *Oh, Great Conqueror endowed with meritorious excellence, glorified with psychic powers and immense fame, transcended all dangers and troubles, and possessed of a special, unique eye, to him may I pay my due respect!!*

After exchanging such a respectful greeting with the Buddha he then informed him of his disciple, Kodhika, who was about to kill himself, and asked him to stop him causing death to his precious life. Obviously, the Buddha knew of Mâra's disguise, so he said to him that the wise do such a thing without attachment to existence. Right at the moment, Kodhika, my son, had uprooted all kinds of craving and entered into final nirvana (extinction without remainder). Immediately after that he together with his many monks left for Kodhika's lodging cottage and seated himself beside his deathbed; whilst Mâra was pondering on Kodhika's consciousness, trying to imagine where it had gone. Then, all of a sudden, he disappeared in the cloudy sky in search for the enlightened monk's consciousness.

Then and there the Buddha told his monks who were standing beside and around him that the evil Mâra was actively looking for Kodhika's consciousness, and that there was no way for him to find his consciousness since he had gone into parinirvana (extinction without remainder, meaning, all the psychophysical components become completely extinguished).

Turning to Mâra who returned to appear to face the Buddha once again after searching in vain, the Buddha rebuked him saying thus:

> *"Oh, Mâra! You would not be able to find Kodhika's consciousness anywhere, in any plane of existence however hard you might try, since he was totally enlightened, utterly wise, endowed with profound wisdom, took a great delight in jhânic meditation, persevered all day and night, had no attachment to existence, conquered the army of death and the snare[31] of life, no more returned to samsaric existence, absolutely uprooted all types of craving and grasping, and entered into parinirvana for good."*

Mâra then, upon hearing such wise words from the Buddha, became frightened and bewildered since it was beyond his expectation and capacity to understand the profundity of consciousness. Therefore, he vanished right there instantaneously. Finally, the Buddha uttered these following words to all his monks thus:

> *Those perfected in discipline and precepts who live their lives with mindfulness and heedfulness, would certainly reach immeasurable freedom, unchangeable emancipation through profound insight. The trace of such persons could never be found by Mâra, the Evil One.*

---

[31] A situation which seems attractive but is unpleasant (even painful) and difficult to escape from---Oxford Dictionary.

Mudra 45

Mudra 45

Mudra of Making the First Monastic Rule

In this mudra the Buddha was seated in the samadhi posture with both hands raised just above his lap and with the open palms slightly facing inward toward his lap and lower abdomen. This implies his manner of making the first monastic rule (disciple, law) for the purpose of protecting his Monastic Order and maintaining the longevity of Buddhasâsana.

Illustrating Story:

The story related to this mudra was rather long with detailed traveling of the Buddha and his meeting with a significant feudalist, Verañja by name, who ruled the large city of Verañjâ, during his stay under the huge tree where also resided a giant called "Naleru", quite close to the city. Herein the author doesn't want to present all those details since they were not really essential, nor were they directly connected to the Buddha's course of laying down his first monastic rule. Nonetheless, the final part of his residing in the above-mentioned place near Verañjâ city was, to some extent, related to his action of making the first rule for his Order of Monks. So, let me share with you, my reader, that part of the story:

After the end of lent observation, the Buddha accompanied by his attendant monk, Ananda, approached Feudalist Verañja at his residence, took the seat prepared for him, and then said to him: *"Oh, Feudalist! We had completed three months of lent observation following your invitation to do so at the vicinity of your city. Now it's time for me and my monks to leave for other State(s)".*

Upon hearing the Buddha's words Verañja became mindful of his invitation, and then confessed to him thus: "*It's true, Most Venerable Master, that I invited you and your monks to pass three months of rainy season here near my city, but had not offered to you all anything worth offering. Then, he ordered his servants to prepare an abundant brunch (breakfast and lunch combined), and offered it to those monks present, headed by the Buddha right there at his mansion.*"

After that the Buddha together with his monks, five hundred in number, took leave of Verañjâ, and traveled randomly without having any destination fixed in his mind. They passed through many places and cities such as Soreyya, Samkassa, Kannakujja, until they reached Payâga city, where there was a harbor in operation. Then and there they crossed the Ganges River and moved forward toward Bârânasi, the capital city of Kâsi State, where they took their temporary residence and stayed as long as they wished. Subsequently, they moved on to Vesâli, the capital city of Vajjî and resided in a huge building called "kûtâgâra" (a building with a peaked roof or pinnacles, possibly gabled; or with an upper storey) situated in an immense forest.

At that time Sudina Kalandaputta, the only son of a millionaire from Kalanda village near Vesâli, after listening to the Buddha's distinguished discourse, became stunningly amazed by it, and therefore wished to join in with his Monastic Order. So, he approached the Great Master asking for the ordination of becoming a monk, to which the Buddha told him about his monastic rule that anyone wanting to become a monk in his Sâsana must get permission from his parents. Therefore, Sudina went back home to ask for his parents' permission, but his father did not want to grant him the permission citing various reasons such as his being his only son, having so much wealth, possessing numerous properties, and needing an inheritant. Overwhelmed by deep grief and disappointment,

Sudina gave up all food consumption (fasting) and thought about joining in with the Buddha's Monastic Order. Eventually, his father gave in, since a good friend of Sudina's convinced him of a tremendous, fatal loss if the permission was not given to his son (he would definitely die). After receiving his father's permission, Sudina returned to the Buddha and got the ordination and became a monk as he wished.

Shortly thereafter, one-day bhikkhu Sudina went to pay a visit with his family, and they were all very happy to see him once again. At an assembly of the family, his father did ask him to disrobe and return to a lay life so that he could manage all the enormous wealth. But Sudina refused to do that which was asked of him. So his father suggested that he produce an inheritant to succeed him. Thinking and pondering thoroughly on the issue concerned, monk Sudina realized that there was no rule prohibiting a monk from having intercourse with a woman, so he reluctantly made love to his former wife for the sole purpose of producing a child at his father's request. In committing such an act he turned out to be so extremely sad and enormously guilty that his fellow monks noticed the state of his emotion, and therefore they inquired into his personal affaires, which he told them honestly and openly what he had done. Then, naturally those monks approached the Great Master and informed him of Sudina's affair with his ex-wife.

As a result, the Buddha summoned to his residence bhikkhu Sudina asking if it was true that he committed a sexual intercourse with his ex-woman, to which the latter confessed with honesty. And then the Buddha ordered all the monks living in the monastery to assemble in a large hall. Then and there the Great Master and Chief of the Monastic Order informed them all of what had happened with bhikkhu Sudina, and therefore he laid down the *first rule* of prohibiting all his monks from having sex with a female entity whether human or otherwise.

The reasons for making any monastic rule laid out by the Buddha were as follows:

1. For beauty of Monastic Order (Community of Monks).
2. For opportuneness of Sangha (Monastic Community).
3. For taming the restless monks and those hard to be disciplined.
4. For orderliness and expediency of those observing precepts with all their hearts.
5. For eliminating the contaminations and intoxications that already occurred.
6. For preventing any contaminations and intoxications from happening in the future.
7. For instigating faith in those who have no faith yet.
8. For increasing faith in those who already have it.
9. For a durable foundation of True Dharma.
10. For supporting and reinforcing the monastic discipline (Vinaya).

Mudra 46

Mudra 46

Mudra of Driving off Monk Vakkali

In this mudra the Buddha was in the samadhi posture with his left hand placed on his lap while raising his right hand to the chest level with the open palm turned inward and the hand's back facing outward. This implies his gesture of driving off or forcing someone, in this case, monk Vakkali, to go away.

Illustrating Story:

In Sâvatthî city there lived a young man, Vakkali by name, born in a wealthy Brahman family, and after having received a good education in liberal arts and sciences he worked in a secure and lucrative job. It happened that one day he saw the Buddha entering the city for collecting alms-food and found the Buddha's body to be beautiful, perfected with all gorgeous and unmatched characteristics, together with a graceful, dignified, admirable, and mindful walking movement. Therefore, he followed the Buddha at a distance, thinking to himself that being a lay person and carrying on the household affairs as he was doing, he would not be able to derive a great benefit from admiring such an attractive physical body as the Buddha's, but being a monk of his Monastic Order should be the way for seeing him closely day and night. For that reason, Vakkali renounced his worldly life together with his enormous wealth and went forth for taking up the monkhood in Buddhasâsana (Dharma and Vinaya).

After joining the Monastic Order, bhikkhu Vakkali did not do any studies in dharma and vinaya (teaching and monastic discipline), nor did he practice any meditation. The only thing of interest to him was the Buddha's physical body, and he did just that: beholding and admiring it at all possible times and in all possible ways by following the Buddha wherever he went. In so doing, he thought he could enjoy seeing the Master's body so much that his sole aim for becoming a monk would be fulfilled.

The Buddha, although he constantly observed bhikkhu Vakkali's behavior, did not say anything but waited patiently for the ripeness of his insight (ñâna) and paramita (perfection) to manifest, to some extent, to his inner eye of wisdom. Once his unmistakable perceptiveness of Vakkali's inner maturity had occurred, the Buddha then gave him this valuable instruction: *"Oh, Vakkali, what do you want from looking at my body? The one who sees Dharma, sees me; he who sees me, sees Dharma. So, behold me (tathâgata) in Dharma. Do not attempt to see tathâgata in his physical body filled with filth and loathsomeness. Why? Because he or she who sees tathâgata in Dharma is considered seeing the Buddha in reality".*

Even though he received such a clear teaching from his Great Master, Vakkali didn't stop following him with an interest in beholding his body. Consequently, the Buddha realized through his profound insight that monk Vakkali would not be able to reach enlightenment if he would not experience sorrow and pain deeply enough. So, one day he told Vakkali to leave his place, and not to appear in front of him any longer thus: *Vakkali! Foolish you!! Get out of here, and do not come to my place anymore. I have had enough of you!!*

Hearing such strong words from the Buddha he took it seriously that the Master had no more compassion for him, and that he lost his refuge entirely and had no more master in whom to take his recourse. With such an unbearable despair and hopelessness, Vakkali decided to commit suicide. He then went to a place where there existed a deep cliff for him to jump over and kill himself. Upon arriving there, he wasted no time but prepared himself for a final jump, first looking down to examine the bottom of the cliff, and then looking up to see its opposite side. Then and there, unexpectedly he saw the Buddha appearing with his compassionate, loving face on the side of the cliff. So, he became startled and could not believe his own eyes. Through his great joy, immense rapture, and deep appreciation for the Buddha's great compassion, Vakkali paid him his highly revered respect and thankfulness from all his heart.

Finally, the Buddha said this to him: *Come! Vakkali, come! Do not be afraid. Behold my body to your utmost satisfaction. I will lift you up from the mass of suffering in which you had sunk just like rescuing an elephant from sinking further into the mud. I will liberate you from pain and suffering, from sorrow and grief, and from samsaric existence to the life of immeasurable freedom and everlasting peace".* Listening attentively and meditatively, Vakkali entered into an acute, great joy, like high waves hitting the shore and producing an uproar of tremendous sounds, that he was almost overwhelmed by it. But through pure mindfulness and vigilant awareness, he managed to calm down that powerful joy (pîti) and turned himself to Vipassana Practice, developing insight and wisdom so intently and continuously that full enlightenment dawned on him together with achievement of special psychic powers right there in front of the cliff and face-to-face with the Buddha.

Mudra 47

Mudra 47

Mudra of Putting Thread In Needle's Hole

In this mudra the Buddha was seated in the samadhi posture with both hands raised to his chest level, and with his left hand holding a needle while his right hand showing an act of putting a thread in the needle's hole.

Illustrating Story:

The Buddha image of this mudra has a significance of demonstrating the Great Master's heart filled with compassion and pure mind full of unconditional, universal love or loving-kindness (mettâ). That is to say, when there was something to get done by a number of monks gathering together, the Buddha always went to preside over the assembly and participate in the activity to be carried out together. He made himself available and easy-going with them all without keeping himself on the throne all the time, so to speak. That was one of the reasons for his monks always to prepare for him his seat at the center of their meeting place, no important if he would come or not. So, they did the same at their gathering for making a robe for Anuruddha Thera. As we will hear the details below:

At one time Anuruddha Thera needed a new robe to replace his old, totally torn one, and he was searching for various pieces of cloth from forest cemeteries, from bushes, and from garbage places where people threw away their unwanted cloths, so as to enable him to put together and make a robe for himself. When his fellow monks knew of his project, they all came over to help him measure, cut, and sew those good pieces into the form of a monk's robe, technically known as "cîvara[32]".

Since it took quite a long while for him to collect enough pieces of cloth to make an upper robe, a devaditâ, Jâlinî by name, who, in one previous life of hers used to be Anuruddha's wife, knew of his difficulty and therefore descended from her heaven, bringing with her a large, beautiful cloth ready for making a robe. She first thought that he would not accept it if she would present it to him directly because in the process of making a monk's robe it's essential that the monk concerned must look for pieces of cloth left unwanted in such places as above-mentioned. So, she hid the main part of that cloth in the soil in a forest, covering it roughly and left other part of it obviously uncovered.

Then, Anuruddha in his search came across the place where the said cloth was hidden and saw it right there on the ground. He pulled it out mindfully and examined it thoroughly realizing that it's a good piece worth making a robe for him. With such a nice piece of cloth in his hands, he returned to his lodging residence and began the process with the assistance of his fellow monks. They measured, cut, and sewed various pieces together in accordance with the design of a cîvara while the Buddha was helping them with putting a thread in the needle's hole, one after the other, so that all the monks present at the gathering could sew conveniently and effectively.

The foregoing story showed us a wonderful example that the Buddha set for a chief of a monastery and/or Sangha Community to follow. He was so friendly, so simple, and so greatly compassionate that his presence provided grace,

---

[32] This is the first of the set of four standard requisites of a Buddhist monk. They are the upper robe (cîvara), alms-bowl (pindapâta), lodging or a place to sleep at (senâsana), and medicinal appliances for use in sickness (gilâna-paccaya-bhesajja-parikkhâra).

inspiration, and encouragement for the work to be carried out lovingly and comfortably. Certainly, it was a work of informal meditation based on mindfulness and insight development supported by mettâ or loving-kindness.

Mudra 48

Mudra 48

Mudra of Transferring Blessings

The Buddha image of this mudra has two distinct forms: One being that the Buddha was seated in the samadhi posture with his left hand placed on his lap while his right hand has its open palm stretched out and rested on his knee. Another form shows the Buddha in his standing posture raising his left hand to the chest level and open palm stretching outward, or lifted up to his shoulder level holding his upper robe, while his right hand was hanging down alongside his body with open palm stretching outward, signaling an act of transferring blessings.

Illustrating Story:

Concerning the Buddha image of this mudra, there were three stories, namely, the blessings given to the medical practitioner Jívaka Komârabhacca, the blessings imparted to bhikkhu Ananda, and the blessings transferred to upâsikâ Visâkhâ. Here the author will relate to our readers only the story of transferring the blessings to upâsikâ Visâkhâ.

At one time the Buddha was spending the rainy season at Jetavana Monastery in the outskirts of Sâvatthî city. Knowing of his taking the residence there, Visâkhâ was extremely happy, and therefore went to see him at the Jetavana botanic garden. The Buddha then gave a proper discourse to her so that she reached a great joy and deepened her dharma practice with diligence and intelligence. Before taking leave of him, she invited him and all his monks residing at Jetavana Monastery at the time to have a meal at her mansion.

The following day a very heavy rain poured down on earth and caused a vastly extended body of water to flood all over the nearby places, including the monastery compound. So the Buddha gave his permission to the monks to bathe themselves in the rain; since no monk had any bathing garment they all took their baths without clothes, which made them look pretty much like naked mendicants.

That morning before the rain fell down, upâsikâ Visâkhâ asked her faithful servant, Cariyâ by name, to go to the monastery to inform the monks of the readiness of the morning meal prepared for them by her mistress. As soon as Cariyâ set out on her trip, the rain fell down very heavily so that she became soaked all over. Upon her arrival at the monastery she saw, according to her perception, only the naked mendicants bathing in the rain enthusiastically, but no monk was seen anywhere in the entire monastery. So, she returned and reported the occurrence to Visâkhâ, and the latter became absolutely surprised hearing such a report, but being well educated, intelligent, and genuinely supportive of the Buddha, Visâkhâ told Cariyâ to go back to the monastery since the rain had stopped, and said to her that by then all the naked mendicants would have left. That time Cariyâ then saw all the monks headed by the Buddha getting ready to leave for her mistress's residence. To Cariyâ the incident appeared like a miracle!!

After the meal, upâsikâ Visâkhâ asked for eight blessings from her Great Master, which he transferred to her after his thorough inquiry into the issue concerned. The following were those eight blessings requested by Maha Upâsikâ Visâkhâ:

"1. May I offer to all the monks bathing garments or vassikasâtaka.
2. May I offer to traveling monks the prepared food for their journeys.
3. May I offer to visiting monks the meals well prepared for them.
4. May I offer to the sick monks the appropriate meals.

5. May I offer to those monks who took care of the sick ones the needed meals.

6. May I offer to the sick monks the medicine and remedy appropriate to their sicknesses.

7. May I offer consistent oatmeal[33] (porridge made from oats) on a regular basis.

8. May I offer to all the bhikkhunis (female monks) the changing clothes for bathing or udakasâtaka to be used for the rest of their lives."

---

[33] In Pali, duvayâgû said to be very rich for nourishing the physical body and maintaining good health.

Mudra 49

Mudra 49

Mudra of Forgiveness

Also, the Buddha image of this mudra exists in two forms: One being that the Buddha was in his standing posture with both hands raised to the chest level and open palms facing outward (resembling the mudra of prohibiting his relatives from waging war). Another form shows the Buddha seated in the samadhi posture raising both hands to his chest level with open palms facing each other and slightly bending forward. This second form is quite well known and therefore is taken as an appropriate mudra of forgiveness.

Illustrating Story:

At one time the Buddha was residing at Ambavana, Jívaka's Mongo Grove, situated in the vicinity of Râjagaha city, capital of Magadha State. At that time Prince Ajátasattu, only son of King Bimbisara, became the ruler of Magadha in succession to his father, but his kingdom was not at peace; instead it turned out to be rather chaotic and obviously disorderly. That was due to three reasons: *First*, he was somewhat young; *second*, he murdered his father in order to succeed the throne; and *third*, he associated himself closely with a badly ambitious monk, Devadatta by name, who was, in fact, the Buddha's cousin but made himself an enemy of the Great Master. For those three reasons, the majority of Magadha citizens did not respect and accept him as their appropriate king.

As a matter of fact, earlier, during his childhood, Prince Ajátasattu was a difficult child, being naughty, disobedient, rebellious, and devastating. Reaching his teens, he became associated with Devadatta, the Buddha's dangerous rival, without his father's knowledge, while King Bimbisâra, his father, was a faithful, devoted supporter of the Buddha. In this way, the young prince established himself as a critical enemy of his own father, and through his belief in and obedience to Devadatta, who always gave him harmful advice, Prince Ajâtasattu became more and more destructive, up to the point of torturing his father to death.

Let us now turn to monk Devadatta for some details. After receiving the ordination for becoming a monk in the Buddha's Monastic Order, he was rather envious of the Great Master as well as of many other monks who came from his royal families since they received more respect and more adoration than he did. With his inferiority complex, he attempted to cause many troubles to the Buddha. For example, he suggested that a rule be set up for all the monks to eat only vegetarian food, which the Buddha refused since it was not practical, given that monks' lives depend on people's generosity and material support, and therefore they must eat whatever was presented to them. The next thing he did was that he approached the Great Master, asking the Buddha to retire and then ro authorize him to be the Monastic Order's new chief, but his request was utterly rejected by the Buddha.

Failing those attempts, Devadatta became so extremely furious that he went up to the Gijjhakûta[34]'s top in the hope of killing the Buddha by pushing a huge stone down to hit him while he was passing by at the mountain's foot. Fortunately, the Buddha did not get severely hurt due to his psychic power of diverting the stone and allowing it to fall beside him so that a small piece of the stone could hit him just perceptibly, causing some injury to his skin.

Later on, Devadatta flew with his supernatural power to King's Ajâtasattu's Grand Palace and descended just in front of him, showing him his great psychic power in order to impress him more, so that the king would continue collaborating with

---

[34] Vulture's Peak.

him until his ultimate goal was achieved. Then, he gave the king a vicious recommendation that he should kill his father and inaugurate himself the king of his kingdom while he himself would go on attempting to get rid of the Buddha and establish himself the topmost chief of the Sangha. Out of his blind ambition and infatuation with power, Ajâtasattu accepted with no reserve Devadatta's recommendation, and went ahead with putting his father in jail, torturing,g and tormenting him by various means and ways. Finally King Bimbisâra, his flesh-and-blood father, died painfully.

Some time later, when King Ajâtasattu reach his mature age, and monk Devadatta entered his fateful death, he realized how destructive he had been, particularly as regards his father who loved and cared for him so much. He then felt an enormous guilt surging through his body and mind, accompanied with tremendous pain and suffering as well as sorrow and grief. So, one day he consulted with his friend, Jîvaka Komârabhacca, a medical doctor and a friend of Ajâtasattu's, regarding a great spiritual master who could help him overcome such a deep suffering. Being a genuine supporter of the Buddha Jîvaka recommended that the king approach the Great Master and ask for help. Ajâtasattu at first was reluctant to follow Jîvaka's wise recommendation due to the fact that he had never met with the Buddha, and that his father when alive admired and worshipped him with all his hearty and mind, but he never paid attention to either his own father or to his Master. Instead, he got into some associations with some significant, so-called spiritual masters who claimed to be perfectly enlightened, but found them all false and fake.

Eventually Jîvaka convinced him of a visit with the Buddha whom he supported and followed his footprint wholeheartedly. Then, both King Ajâtasattu and Doctor Jîvaka went to see the Buddha at Ambavana, his mango grove, and the king told him all his personal stories including his close association with monk Devadatta and his vicious action of ordering his father to be jailed, tortured, and tormented to death. As a result, he suffered unbearable pain and irreversible guilt, and therefore came for help from the Great Master of the whole world.

After relating to the Buddha all his deeds concerning his association with such a bad monk, Devadatta, and his evil, unforgivable action of causing death to his father, the righteous king, the dharma king, who ruled over Magadha Kingdom with wisdom, love, compassion, prudence, and benevolence, Ajâtasattu then requested pardon and forgiveness from the Buddha so that he would be relieved from such a deep grief and excruciating suffering.

Out of compassion and empathy for King Ajâtasattu who confessed honestly and openly his evil, destructive deeds committed, and who at the same time realized the truth as regards his father, the Buddha accepted his humble request and said to him: *"Oh, Great King! I acknowledge your evil action and painful remorse (guilt) resulted from it. The person who has committed evil, and then realized his utterly wrong doing, confessed it honestly and openly to a Spiritual Master like Tathâgata[35], and promises not to commit such an evil action once and for all, is considered a righteous person in Dharma and Vinaya of the Tathâgata."* Then and there he granted the pardon to King Ajâtasattu and blessed him with peace, light, and universal love.

After expressing his heartfelt thanks to the Buddha and his complete acceptance of the Great Master as his only Spiritual Mentor, King Ajâtasattu took leave of him. Right after that, the Buddha told his monks present at the gathering thus: *"Monks! King Ajâtasattu overcame by his evil action and its painful*

---

[35] Another title of the Buddha. He often refers to himself as such.

consequences; if he would not have caused undue death to his father, the righteous King, he could have reaped the Noble Fruition of Entering the Eternal Flow of Nirvanic Current right here at his seat in front of Tathâgata."

Upon hearing those wise words uttered by the Buddha those monks reached great joy and deep appreciation altogether.

Mudra 50

Mudra 50

Mudra of Subduing King Jambûpati
or
Mudra of Dressing in Monarch's Royal Garments

In this mudra the Buddha was seated in the samadhi posture with his left hand opened upwards and placed on his lap, while his right arm was extended, its palm placed downwards, resting on his right knee (similar to the mudra of conquering Mâra). Since the Buddha image of this mudra was dressed up in a monarch's royal garments, it's very so often named in accordance with such attire.

Illustrating Story:

Since the story is quite long and filled with a variety of magic and numerous miracles performed by both King Jambûpati and the Buddha, to the author it appears rather delusory and superstitious, like a legend or folk tale. Therefore, he will not go into details but summarize the story as follows:

It was said that during the Buddha's initial epoch there lived in Pañcâla city King Jambûpati with his Queen Kâñcanâ. He was quite a meritorious and powerful king since he possessed a magical weapon called "visa kandaka, "meaning "poisonous arrow," and had shoes made of special gems, and held a wand of magical gem. With those three magical weapons he conquered many small countries in his neighborhood, but did not feel satisfied with his enormous wealth, his utmost power, and his vastly superior sovereignty. So, one day he put on his magic shoes and carried in his right hand his powerful magic wand and flew in the skies, traveling by air and inspecting various cities and countries on earth from above. Eventually he reached the sky of Râjagaha, the capital city of Magadha Super Power State, looking down and seeing a huge palace illuminated with bright lights and various, distinctive colors. To him it was the most beautiful place, which he had never seen in his life, so he at first hit it with his both feet with his shoes on, but the palace's roof remained as solid as ever and did not get damaged even slightly. Then, with fury he threw his magic wand toward the royal grand palace of King Bimbisâra, the ruler of Magadha State, although he did not know to whom the palace belonged. As a result, his wand got crooked and became ineffective and useless in hitting the palace. Consequently, he returned home to Pañcâla city with an unwavering determination to destroy such a wonderful and most valuable palace together with all its precious belongings.

Fortunately, King Bimbisâra was not in the palace at the time of King Jambûpati attacking it, but was having an audience with the Buddha, his Great Master, conversing with him on the matter of Dharma and the ways and means to tackle certain problematic situations. Later, he received a full report on what had happened to his palace from his aides and security secretary, and therefore he asked the Buddha for protection and safety, which the latter promised to do all necessary things to protect the king's life, his people, and his properties. As we know, the Buddha can get anything done safely and successfully using his psychic and supernatural powers when the situation calls for. The same was applied to the grave situation between King Jambûpati, the attacker, and King Bimbisâra, the defender.

Now, let us return to King Jambûpati who was then residing in his palace much inferior to that of King Bimbisâra's. Because of burning envy and fury he sent his poisonous arrow or visa kandaka by air to destroy the Magadha State King's most beautiful palace on earth together with all its properties. To his dismay and agony the most powerful magic wand of his could not do anything effective, worse still, it turned out to be broken up into pieces. So he himself set out a trip to Magadha Super Power State aiming for crutching King Bimbisâra and his palace as well as for seizing and occupying his capital city, Râjagaha.

Instead of going into the battlefield with him, Righteous King of Magadha State took refuge under his Great Master's protection at Veluvana Monastery where he resided at that time.

It was very interesting that the Buddha psychically and miraculously turned himself into a Great King and all his monks together with his nuns and lay devotees into solders of armed forces, ready to fight a war with King Jambûpati who came for the sole purpose of making war. But the war that they (Buddha and Jambûpati) carried out was the psychic power war, and not a material, physical war. They exchanged their magic powers in various forms, but King Jambûpati lost all his magic weapons since they were neither effective nor functional in materializing their powers, instead they succumbed to the Buddha's psychic powers in every form and every time during their psychic and magical fighting.

Finally, King Jambûpati surrendered unconditionally, and then the Buddha turned himself back to being Buddha and all his so-called soldiers returned to become whoever they were before, and therefore no more existed the seemingly armed forces. Then the Great Master of the world delivered a distinguished discourse for purifying King Jambûpati's unskilful, filthy, and destructive mind and for transforming him at all levels of his human realities. At the end of his eloquent sermon King Jambûpati reached the initial but irreversible enlightenment and asked for joining in with his Monastic Order, which the Buddha gave with his mega mettâ and infinite compassion.

๕๑

Mudra 51

Mudra 51

Mudra of Pâlileyyaka[36] Jungle

In this mudra the Buddha seated himself on a rock with both feet placed lightly on the ground while his left hand with its palm down rested on his left thigh and his right hand with its palm up reposed on his right knee. This is a gesture of reception (receiving something) and is well known as "mudra of Pâlileyyaka jungle". In Thailand the Buddha image of this mudra is popularly worshipped by those born on Wednesday night and those reaching the age governed by the planet Saturn, astrologically speaking.

Illustrating Story:

At one time the Buddha was staying at Ghositârâma Monastery in Kosambî city, and encountered a certain number of monks difficult to teach and to guide with regard to discipline and practice of monastic rules since they were quarrelsome and disobedient. Although he tried his best to help them cultivate mindfulness in daily living and realize the significance of respect and acceptance, he failed in all ways and means. Those two dharmas that bring about inner beauty and grace to their practitioners, which the Buddha attempted to impart to them, were not in their interest and attention at all. The two dharmas are *khanti*: patience, and *soracca*: calmness and graciousness.

Failing to discipline and guide those haughty and conceited monks of Kosambî, the Buddha left for Rakkhitavana (protected forest) to live in solitude and in peace by himself. During the three months of his residence in such a tranquil,

---

[36] It's the name of a great elephant that rendered its services to the Buddha during his stay in solitude for three months in a protected forest.

pleasant, and quiet thick forest or jungle, a great elephant called Pâlileyyaka who also left its herd for the very similar reasons, rendered its services and took care of the Buddha's material necessities. At the same time, an intelligent monkey overwhelmed by the Great Master's grace, auspiciousness, and delightful energy, nourished him with a hive of honey on a regular basis (as appeared in the picture). So, since the elephant and the monkey looked after his needs and fulfilled all his fundamental requirements, he did not need to go out for alms-food in any village, which was extremely far away from the jungle where he stayed. Needles to say, the Buddha was quite happy and comfortable the Buddha was.

After the Buddha's abandonment of those disobedient and wicked monks, they encountered troubles: the people who followed the Buddha and his Sâsana boycotted them by not giving them any kind of food and drinks, let alone a provision of their basic requisites. They forced those monks to go and ask for pardon from their Great Master, but Rakkhitavana was extremely far away from Kosambî city and also as it was the season for observing lent, they could not go to pass a night anywhere else outside of their monastery, Ghositârâma by name. As a result, they suffered a great deal during their three-month-observance of lent.

After the lent season was over, those significant followers and supporters of the Buddha such as the millionaire Anâthapindika and the Great Upâsikâ Visâkhâ sent their messages to bhikkhu Ananda, the Buddha's attendant monk, requesting that he invite the Great Master on their behalf to return to Sâvatthî. Also, a great number of monks living in various countryside lodges came over to Ananda and presented to him the same request: an invitation extended to the Buddha to return to a city monastery so that they could have some audiences with him and receive his wise advice and listen to his articulate dharma talks.

Eventually those good monks headed by Ananda went to see their Great Master in the deep jungle of Rakkhitavana. Arriving at the edge of that jungle, Ananda paused for a short while and thought to himself that it would be inappropriate to lead all the monks to the Buddha's residence since it might disturb the peaceful and silent atmosphere of his place. So, he asked them to wait there while he went in alone quietly, and after paying proper respects to him, humbly informed him of the wishes of his monks and lay followers to see him in a city monastery, for example, Jetavana Vihara in Sâvatthî. The Buddha then asked if he came alone, to which Ananda replied that he was accompanied by many monks, five hundred in number, who were awaiting at the edge of Rakkhitavana jungle since he thought that if they all entered the jungle together there would be some disturbance and distraction unnecessarily caused to the serenely tranquil and quiet atmosphere of the wonderful jungle. But with the Buddha's grant of permission, Ananda took his temporary leave of him to bring those monks in, and when they all arrived at his simple but delightful[37] residence, they paid their proper respect by prostrating before him three times and then took their seats in suitable places surrounding him.

Then and there he told them about his solitary but pleasant and delicious life in Rakkhitavana supported sufficiently and comfortably by the blessed elephant Pâlileyyaka and occasionally by the great monkey who provided him with honey. He pointed out clearly that living together must be based on friendship and companionship, as in his living a harmonious life with the blessed Pâlileyyaka, the commendable monkey, and all animals, reptiles, insects, trees, and plants in the entire jungle. He further said to them that *whoever has a good, noble*

---

[37] In Pali, ramaniya: delightful, charming, beautiful, and auspicious.

friend who is knowledgeable³⁸, well developed, constantly mindful, and wise to share his or her life with in the form of promising companionship, can live a great life, the noble life of wholeness. Failing to find such a friend, it would be better to live alone ("all-one: being one with all and not feeling lonely, although physically alone). At the end of his flowing remarks, all the monks present in front of him realized the truth of nirvana and attained to perfect enlightenment since they were all ripened and matured enough for it, just like a lotus flower rising above the water, waiting for the sun to help it reach its full blossom.

Right after that, Ananda Thera informed the Buddha of the wishes of those noble devotees, five millions in number, led by Anâthapindika, the millionaire of Sâvatthî, on the men's side, and Mahâ Upâsikâ Visâkhâ, the most benevolent and wealthy devotee, on the women's side. They all sent their humble messages to invite him to their city so that they could see him and listen to his discourses on dharma. Upon hearing that, he told Ananda to prepare the trip, and he then set out his journey with those five hundred monks accompanied by the blessed elephant Pâlileyyaka, his devoted provider.

Upon their arrival at the human frontier where human villages were situated, the Buddha talked compassionately and thankfully to Pâlileyyaka that he had done all possible meritorious deeds, looking after his material needs to his best capacity, for which he appreciated deeply. He further told him that although he could not achieve a meditative absorption (jhâna) and develop insight and wisdom (Vipassana) in this life time due to being an animal and lacking fully equipped faculties for doing that, he had planted a fertile seed of enlightenment during his three-month services rendered to him wholeheartedly and industriously, he would become one of the

---

[38] This refers to understanding perfectly and seeing in profound wisdom, as well as experiencing with pure awareness.

Mudras of the Buddha (His Life and Works)   215

enlightened people in the future, when his human form would be materialized. Thus saying the Buddha blessed Pâlileyyaka once more and then let him return to the jungle, his homeland where he belonged, and then continued his own travel toward Sâvatthî city.

Now about the naughty, conceited monks of Kosambî: upon hearing that the Buddha had returned to Jetavana Monastery in Sâvatthî, they were happy and therefore left for the monastery in hope of asking for pardon and forgiveness from the Great Master. First, they encountered a big problem in entering Sâvatthî because King Pasenadi, Great King of Kosala Super Power State of which Sâvatthî was the capital, did not want to have them in his city due to their unethical and unwelcoming behavior expressed to their Great Master, the Buddha whom the king supported with all his heart and mind and held his highly revered respect to. Knowing of such a difficulty the Buddha intervened by requesting King Pasenadi to give them his entry permission so that they could come in and confess their gravely erroneous ethical conduct and ask for pardon from Tathâgata, their proper Master. With his compassionate intervention, they got the king's authorization to enter Sâvatthî and came to pay their appropriate respects to the Buddha at Jetavana Vihara.

At the monastery, the Buddha gave his order to the receptionist monk to arrange a certain place for the Kosambî monks to stay separately and without mixing them with the rest of resident monks of Jetavana Vihara. So, none of those resident monks would sit or stand or communicate with the Kosambî monks, which was a form of ex-communication. The Buddha then summoned all his monks to gather together at the assembly hall, letting those monks from Kosambî sit on one side and the resident monks sit opposite to them. There he pointed his finger to the haughty Kosambî monks saying how arrogant and badly disobedient they were during his stay with them at Ghositârâma in Kosambî, and further telling them that they created a schism in the Sangha and destroyed the unity and harmony in living together, which was considered a most severely bad karma ever to be committed by anyone in his Dharma and Vinaya. After thus saying, he pardoned them and asked all resident monks to accept and welcome them on friendly terms and with their warm hearts as well as their understanding minds. In this way, all the monks were united and lived together in peace and in harmony ever after.

Finally the Great Master of the globe delivered his discourse to all the monks, the nuns, and lay devotees who were present at a massive gathering as follows:

While we were suffering a grave destruction, the others did not feel how bad it was for us. But, when some members of the community realized the damages and destructiveness being done to their community as a whole, then their disputes and quarrels would end in a realistic solution because of the right practice adopted and carried out by them all together.

It always happened at the end of his eloquent discourse that all the matured monks present at the assembly realized the truth of nirvana and became enlightened.

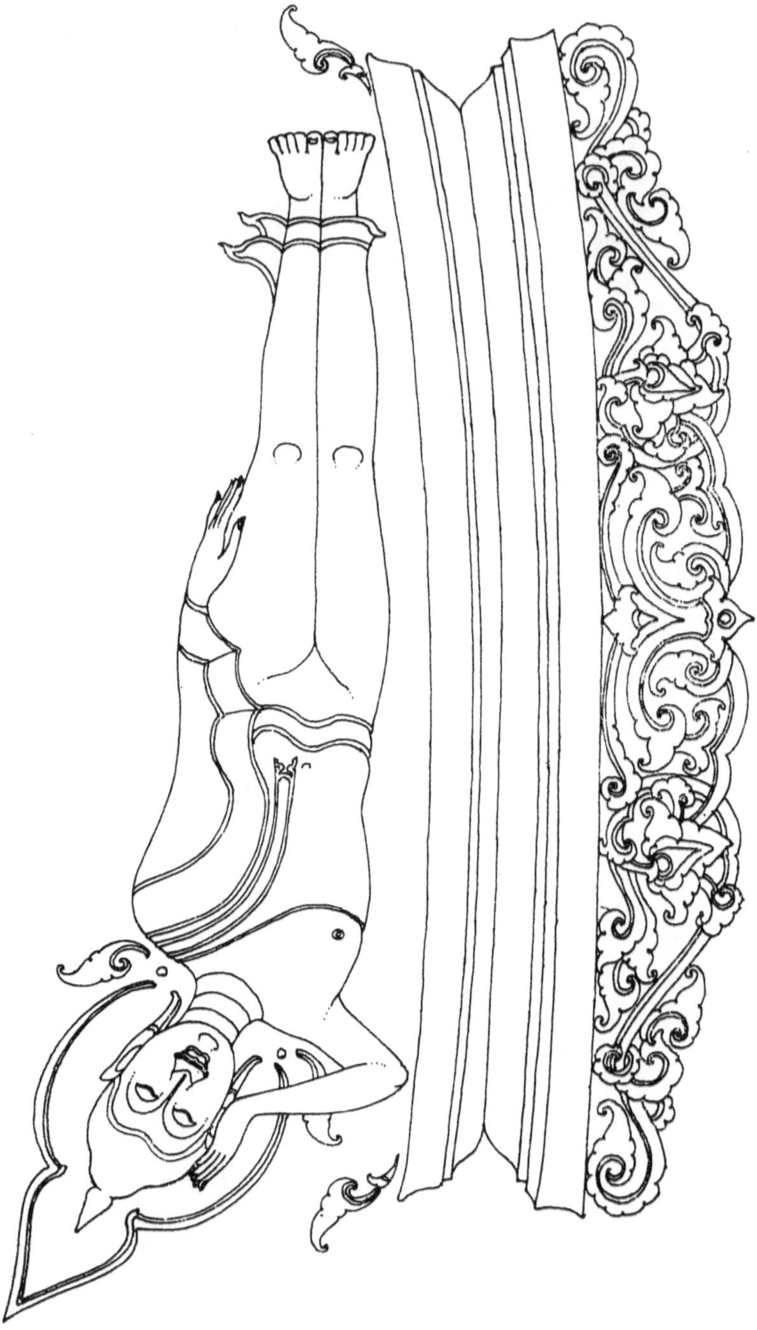

Mudra 52

Mudra 52

Mudra of Setting Free Asurindarâhu[39]

In this mudra the Buddha was in the lying or reclining on-his-right-side posture[40] with his left foot resting on his right foot in total equilibrium while his left hand stretched alongside his body and reposed on it comfortably, his right armpit placed on the pillow and his right hand raised, the forearm raised from the elbow, with the Buddha resting on the right hand that supports his head with its open palm.

Illustrating Story:

At one time the Buddha was residing at Jetavana Monastery in Sâvatthî, and at that time Asurindarâhu (viceroy to King Vepacitti Asurâdhipati, great king of the titans, named Vepacitti), the ruler of asura kingdom, heard of the Buddha's reputation and fame that he was a Perfectly Enlightened Master, endowed with knowledge and ethical conduct, the world-realizer, the incomparable trainer of human beings, devas, and brahmas, and the Great Master with utterly awakened heart

---

[39] Chief or king of Titans. Several Asuras (Titans) are accredited with the role of leaders, most commonly Vepacitti and Râhu. The Asuras, the Titans, are a class of mythological beings, and are classed with other inferior deities such as nâgâ (mythological serpents), yakkhâ (giants), garujâ (mythological huge and powerful birds), and so on. Also, rebirth as an Asura is considered as one of the four unhappy planes of existence or evil fates after death; they are apâya or niraya (hell), tiracchâna-yoni (animal kingdom), petâ (hungry ghosts), and asura (titans). The fight between gods and titans is also reflected in the oldest books of Pali Canon and occurs in identical description at passages under the title of devâsura-sangâma. *The Pali Text Society's Pali-English Dictionary*, 2004.
[40] In Pali, sihaseyyâsa. Also visit Wat Po in Bangkok, Thailand, to see the gigantic reclining Buddha image there.

filled with great joy and full bloom. Therefore, he wanted to pay a visit to the Buddha, but thought to himself that he (Buddha) was a human being with a small physical body in comparison with him who possessed a gigantic body, and for that reason he would have to bend his head down in bowing when looking at the Buddha, which he would have never done as the king of titans (asuras). So he paused and thought again and again a few times, and eventually he made up his mind to go for his visit with the Great Master of the Globe. Before his arrival, the Buddha told Ananda, his attendant monk, to prepare a welcome site in the large compound of his gandhaguti (lodging house) by laying out an enormous bed on which he would lie down, showing the manner of receiving Asurindarâhu. Then he created through his supernatural, psychic power an immense body reclining on such a large bed with vigilance, mindfulness, and serene calmness, waiting for the arrival of the Titans' King.

As soon as he arrived, Asurindarâhu saw with amazement the Buddha's huge body, ten times more than his own. He couldn't believe his eyes! Then, the Buddha exchanged his heartfelt, welcome greetings with him saying thus:

Oh, Asurindarâhu! Those hearing a hearsay without seeing and witnessing with their own eyes whatever they have heard about, and with no thorough examinations, should not praise or blame it. Asurindarâhu! In fact, those asuras in your kingdom have much smaller bodies than yours. Don't you think that in other planes of life there would be some beings with their bodies much bigger than yours? Asurindarâhu! You might have maintained the view that your physical body is the largest one in the whole universe just like a big fish that lives in a pond and see only small fishes, without experiencing an ocean in which many large fishes exist and carry out their lives.

To show him the higher plane of life where the brahmas with their massive bodies live, the Buddha took him there. Upon seeing and viewing those gigantic bodies of living brahmas who came to pay their proper respect to the Buddha, Asurindarâhu got so frightened and was trembled all over his body that he hid himself behind the Great Master since he felt himself as tiny as a spider hanging on its net. In turn, the Buddha comforted him and calmed him down with his caring and loving words.

Witnessing perceptively such an episode, Mahâ Brahma, chief of the brahma world, asked the Buddha what was it that he brought with him in his upper robe, to which the Buddha replied that it was Asurindarâhu, who claimed to have a huge body, and who wanted to see if there would be any being in the entire universe that had an enormous body either equal to his own body or much greater than his. Therefore, the Tathâgata brought him to see for himself the gigantic bodies that the brahmas possessed. Responding to the Great Master's statement, Mahâ Brahma remarked that a person thick with self-conceit and self-aggrandizement always held such an idea that he or she was better, bigger, and more important than others, just as a poor person upon receiving a certain amount of money worth a hundred dollars or so would consider himself/herself as a wealthy one, or a foolish man or woman who happened to have some knowledge would elevate himself/herself to a position of being a learned, knowledgeable one because of his/her chief feature of ego-centricity.

After his appropriate stay in the brahma plane of existence, the Buddha took leave of Mahâ Brahma and his retinue and guided Asurindarâhu back to Jetavana Vihara. Then and there he further subdued Asurindarâhu up to the point that he became emancipated from his chief feature of self-importance and ego-conceit together with his erroneous, pernicious view on life and on personality, and therefore was transformed at all levels of his realities whether psychological, emotional, mental, and spiritual. At the end of the Buddha's remarks on the distinguished dharma, Asurindarâhu turned out to be greatly enthusiastic and deeply appreciative of his brief but meaningful dharma talk, and immediately asked for refuge in the Great Master, in his Dharma, and in his Noble Sangha, which the Buddha granted him with illimitable mettâ and boundless compassion. Soon after that, he took leave of the Great Master and of the immeasurably peaceful monastery, and returned to his plane of asura existence.

Mudra 53

Mudra 53

Mudra of Converting Âlavaka Yakkha

In this mudra the Buddha seated in the samadhi posture with his left hand opened up and placed on his left knee while his right hand lifted up to the chest level and fingers slightly bent inward, indicating the gesture of teaching.

Illustrating Story:

In the middle of a forest, not far from the city of Álaví, there lived a gang of man-eaters, or Yakkhas[41], that caused terrible problems for the citizens of Álaví. The citizens tried to destroy the Yakkhas by all conceivable means, but without success; only managing to suppress them temporarily. The Yakkhas were very cruel and loved to eat all kinds of live animals and human beings. The Yakkhas captured and ate anyone that happened into the forest.

One day, the Monarch of Álaví went into the forest on horseback to hunt. Chasing a wild animal, he entered the area where the man-eaters lived and was captured. The Yakkhas wanted to eat him immediately, but they were stayed by his negotiations. He promised to send them his citizens for their food, if they would let him go. The man-eaters, having received the good end of the bargain, liberated the Monarch, warning that if he did not fulfil the agreement then he would become their meal.

---

[41] This term "Yakkha" literally means "giant," but in the context used in the Buddhist literature, Yakkha refers to a certain tribe that is very cruel and merciless, and lives in a forest. Their body type and general appearance is similar to an average human being.

Trouble spread across the kingdom. Everyone's safety was threatened constantly, and nobody knew when he or she was going to be delivered to the Yakkhas. Prisoners were the first to become victims of the horrible accord that their Monarch had made with the man-eaters. After a time, almost all the prisoners disappeared from the prisons and those being jailed became fewer and fewer. The population of the man-eating gang grew quickly, and they all greatly enjoyed human flesh. The next victims were the orphaned, the poor, and the handicapped. Those wandering in a solitary place would be caught by the secret police, for the purpose of supplying the terrible forest gang. Many people escaped and abandoned their property, and even the kingdom, in order to save their lives and the lives of their children. Eventually, the city of Álaví was almost deserted due to the great danger of the cruel Yakkhas and the stupidity of their Monarch.

The entire land was ablaze with the news of the horrendous trouble that oppressed the people of Álaví Kingdom. The Buddha decided to help and went alone directly to speak to the forest gang, to stop them from doing these terrible things. His disciples found it difficult to comprehend why he went alone, since the situation was very dangerous and risky. The Yakkhas had no mercy in their hearts and minds for anyone at all.

The Buddha arrived at the camp of the Yakkhas, where he was forbidden to enter by the guards, who said to him that if he reached the head of their gang, he would be eaten. But the Buddha was determined to meet and talk with the gang leader, so he asked for permission to go in and do what he had come to do. Finally, the guards let him in. However, their leader, Âlavaka, was not there. The Buddha decided to wait by seating himself with dignity and courage in an armchair that belonged to Âlavaka.

When he returned, Âlavaka saw the Buddha sitting there in his armchair and became furious. Âlavaka knew that the monk who came to his place was not an ordinary monk, but a Supreme Buddha whom numerous people, including kings and princes of various states, admired and respected highly. Nevertheless, he shouted at the Buddha, saying, "Get out!" The Buddha did not respond with resistance, but rather followed his order. Then Âlavaka ordered him again, "Come back in!" The Buddha returned with no hesitation. He then gave another command, "Get out!" The Buddha conformed to his command and went out. Now Âlavaka said to him, "Sit down!" Buddha simply sat down. Âlavaka gave the last order, saying, "Stand up!" The Buddha stood up immediately.

Âlavaka Yakkha was astonished at the Buddha's conformity to these orders. Âlavaka thought, "Why does the great monk like the Buddha receive these orders so easily?"

The Buddha observed that Âlavaka Yakkha enjoyed his control and manipulation exceedingly well, and he said to Âlavaka, "Enough, Âlavaka! If you want to punish me or kill me, do so without reservation."

Instead, Âlavaka responded, "Monk, I would like to ask you some questions. If you are able to answer them, do so. If not, you will have to die."

The Buddha wanted to demonstrate his inner knowledge to the Yakkha, and countered with this question: "Yakkha, do you still remember the questions, those questions that you received from your grandfather?" Âlavaka responded affirmatively.

Then the Buddha told him to hurry up, as he was very eager to answer him. After that, Âlavaka put these questions to the Buddha, who answered in turn:

"What is the priceless human treasure?"
"Honesty[42] is the highest treasure."
"How can one achieve happiness?"
"By living the Dharmic (Righteous) life."
"What is the most flavourful thing?"
"Honesty is the most flavourful thing."
"What kind of life is the best?"
"The life endowed with Mindfulness and Wisdom is indeed the best."

After these questions and answers, the Buddha continued conversing with Âlavaka Yakkha for a while. As a result, the Great Yakkha admitted his wrongdoing and stopped harming all human beings. Since then peace, freedom, happiness, and prosperity prevailed throughout Álaví Kingdom.

---

[42] Here it implies "purity of heart".

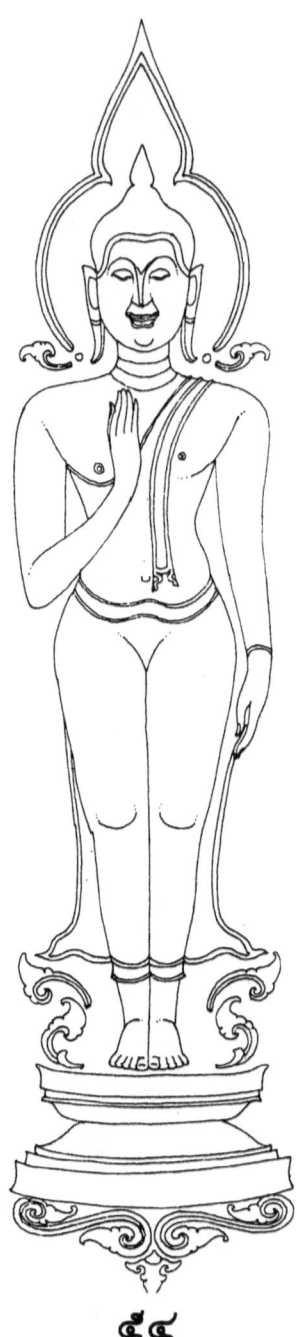

Mudra 54

Mudra 54

Mudra of Subduing the Robber Angulimâla

In this mudra the Buddha was in his standing posture with his left hand hanging down and his right hand raised to the chest level with its palm pointing toward the left side.

Illustrating Story:

This story begins in the land of Kosala, which was ablaze with trouble caused by a robber named Angulimâla. Citizens across the kingdom lived with tremendous fear and anxiety, especially those residing in the rural countryside. Many abandoned their homes and migrated into towns and cities, to escape Angulimâla. Angulimâla was known to kill without mercy or discrimination. When the situation became utterly critical, the government made a national announcement and informed all its citizens that they had to take serious precautions. The armed forces would mobilize troops to crush the merciless, fierce robber. Hearing the plan, Angulimâla's mother, Mantání, became extremely worried about her son's fate. She decided to risk her life by making a long journey from home, in the hope of finding her son in a prohibited region in the deep forest.

At the same time, the Buddha made up his mind to go and have a talk with Angulimâla. He went by himself, without any monks accompanying him. Angulimâla was roaming about looking for someone to kill, and the Buddha went straightaway in Angulimâla's direction.

Everything went exactly the way the Buddha expected. The moment Angulimâla glanced at the Buddha, Angulimâla ran toward him in the hope of killing him and cutting off his finger. Angulimâla's goal was to present one thousand fingers to his teacher in exchange for learning a very special mantra, as the teacher had promised. Angulimâla only needed one more finger!

With the sword stained with human blood in his hand, Angulimâla ran as quickly as he could towards the Buddha, but never could Angulimâla get close enough to strike the Buddha with his sword! While Angulimâla was running at his full speed, the Buddha was just walking leisurely. Even so, Angulimâla could not catch up with him. The story tells us that Angulimâla ran after the Buddha for about forty-eight kilometers, or for three yojanas, according to the ancient system of calculation.

At this point Angulimâla became exhausted. He didn't have much more energy left to run further, and then he called out loudly to the Buddha, "Monk! Stop!"

"I have stopped, but you yourself haven't stopped," responded the Buddha, while still walking.

Becoming furious, Angulimâla shouted once more, "You are a liar, monk! You have not stopped, yet you say you have stopped."

Then, the Buddha answered him, saying, "Being a monk, I do not speak a lie. I have stopped doing all evil things. What about yourself, when are you going to stop killing?"

Having heard the Buddha's wise response, Angulimâla suddenly threw away his sword, and took out the garland of human fingers that he wore around his neck and flung them all into the bushes. Upon witnessing his radical change, the Buddha waited for a short time, and then preached the Dharma to Angulimâla, until eventually Angulimâla asked for ordination as a monk, and to join with the Buddha for life.

Actually, Angulimâla's life story is much more detailed, but here we are considering the specific part that concerns the

Buddha's role in transforming him, so that we may learn how his great success generated a sudden change in Angulimâla.

It is evident that the Buddha won over Angulimâla by using a supernatural power. That is to say, the Buddha allowed Angulimâla to run after him at Angulimâla's fastest speed, but Buddha did not allow Angulimâla to catch up with him. There are two reasons that the Buddha chose to demonstrate his supernatural power in this way.

First, the Buddha used his supernatural power to defeat Angulimâla's great physical force. Criminals are generally infatuated with their physical strength. They believe they have enormous power over everyone else. When criminals lose their physical power, they are much more easily overcome. Mentally they may still be hateful and cruel, but they become discouraged quickly when their physical strength does not support them. For this reason, killers often look for followers or trainees as a substitute for their concrete physical power.

Angulimâla was a solitary killer, a single swordsman. Before encountering the Buddha, Angulimâla had not eaten for several days, as he had been occupied compulsively collecting a thousand human fingers from his victims. Angulimâla himself was on the brink of exhaustion. The Buddha's method of subduing Angulimâla was to make him lose his last bit of physical strength by sprinting some forty-eight kilometers. Although Angulimâla was a remarkable runner, his stamina ultimately failed, which caused him to stop and to stand still.

The second reason the Buddha decided to show his supernatural power was to demonstrate that a True Master does not demand killing. Remember that Angulimâla adopted a killer's behavior, and collected dead people's fingers at the instigation of his teacher. This teacher deceived Angulimâla shamelessly, telling Angulimâla that he would give him secret knowledge and the most powerful mantra, upon completion of this quest to obtain a thousand fingers from those whom he killed -- one finger from each person. Angulimâla was terribly unfortunate to have such a teacher, who wanted to be Angulimâla's undoing. Many valuable subjects were energetically pursued by thousands of other interested people in his time.

Angulimâla, in fact, was the only son of good parents and a respectable family. He was intelligent, industrious, humble, and kind. His father was a Counselor to the King of Kosala Country, King Pasenadi. Being ardent believers in education, his parents presented him to a well-known teacher in Takkasila, far away from Sávatthí, the capital of Kosala, where they lived. Angulimâla, whose real name was Ahimsaka (non-violent one), was a very good student and learned quickly any subject exposed to him. In addition, he possessed a kind, polite, and affable manner, and therefore became a favorite of his teacher and family. As a result, he became the object of jealousy and envy for many of his classmates.

It is quite common that a good, popular, and successful person becomes a target of jealousy for those surrounding him/her. Angulimâla (or Ahimsaka as he was then known) was no exception. Nasty and indolent students, who were only squandering their parent's money, instead of honestly pursuing an education, ruthlessly accused him of being the secret lover of the teacher's wife. Tending to be a nervous and suspicious character, the teacher believed the accusation to be true without pondering the matter very deeply. He came up with a dirty plan to eliminate Angulimâla. The teacher devised a cruel ruse. Angulimâla was to collect a thousand human fingers from those whom he killed with his own hands, so that he would be able to learn a special mantra which would help him become a great, mighty and famous person.

At first, Ahimsaka could not accept his teacher's instruction, because it was against his conscience and in conflict with his will, but under his teacher's insistence and compelling force, Ahimsaka finally succumbed. We must consider him to be an unfortunate young man who had a bad karma, in the sense of having the most terrible teacher whom anyone might ever encounter.

Everyone should bear in mind that a fake and false Guru can do a great deal of psychological, mental, and spiritual harm to his/her disciples, particularly if the disciples are convinced that the Guru is an enlightened master, and can do no wrong and no harm. Be aware, awake, and vigilant at all times, and quick to grasp the real meaning of that to which you are being exposed!

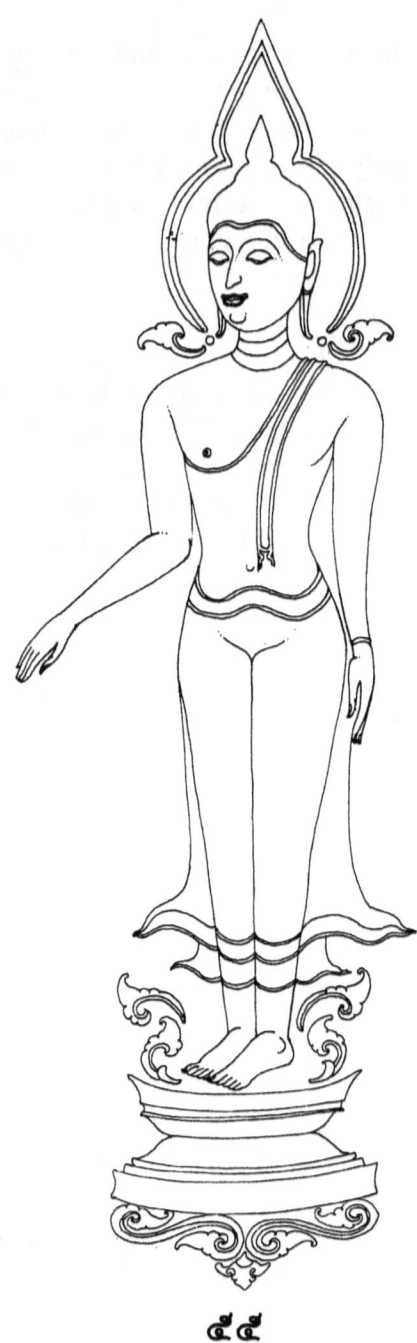

Mudra 55

Mudra 55

Mudra of Taming the Elephant Nâlâgiri

In this mudra the Buddha was his standing posture with his left hand hanging down by his side and his right arm by his side with the forearm stretching forward at the level of his belly with the palm opened downward toward the earth. This indicates the manner of stroking Nâlâgiri's head with mettâ (illimitable, universal love) at the moment when the elephant was approaching him and bowing at the Buddha's feet.

Illustrating Story:

The story of the Nâlâgiri elephant was related to the monk Devadatta and the Crown Prince Ajâtasattu, the royal son of King Bimbisâra of Magadha State. Plotting to destroy the Buddha, Devadatta persuaded Ajâtasattu to kill his father, the King of Magadha. (See here the story given with Mudra 49.)

Devadatta was a cousin of the Buddha, and it is not clear why Devadatta joined the Buddha's monastic order. Perhaps he wanted to stay close to the Buddha, in order to have a better chance to bring about the Buddha's destruction. However, he may have had the pure intention of eliminating his mental contaminations, according to the goal of monkhood set forth by the Buddha. Devadatta's reason for becoming a monk was not as obvious as that of the other princes -- who were clearly intending to follow the Buddha faithfully with their devotional hearts.

Devadatta's behaviour after his ordination indicated that he was ambitiously seeking a position of leadership in the Sangha and in the Buddha's inner circle. He was quite competitive with the Buddha in many respects, although he carried this out very subtly.

Despite wearing the saffron robe, Devadatta's deeply rooted tendency from adolescence to lead a gang of men did not decrease. He encountered a dissatisfying situation day after day, the interest that the lay Buddhists showed to his fellow monks. No one ever asked to see him or paid attention to him. Those coming to the monastery always asked for Bhikkhu Ánanda, the Venerable Sáriputta or some other monk, but never Devadatta. As a matter of fact, he never received any invitation from anyone at all. Poor Devadatta! His fate was to be only a monk who helped people with offerings in their hands to find the way to other monks' dwelling places.

This situation did not help him realize the consequences of his bad karma. That is to say, he did not become aware of the wrongs that he had committed before joining the Monastic Order, nor had he made any efforts to reach the higher path and the fruition of the Dharma practice, including the realization of Nirvana. Instead, he took the dissatisfactory situation as an excuse for finding a way to commit even worse karma, because of his wrong reasoning that he could triumph over his personal evil karma by creating more evil things in life.

Then Devadatta conceived the idea that the Buddha had became famous and had received rich offerings from people all over the Jambúdípa, only because of Bimbisára, the Great King of the Magadha State. In order to destroy the Buddha, it seemed essential to Devadatta that King Bimbisára must first be eliminated. Just like a tree or a plant cannot exist without water and nutrition, the Buddha would not flourish without the king!

Nevertheless, to put King Bimbisára out of the picture was not an easy job. He was greatly loved by his people all over the kingdom. But there was a way, and that was to prompt the king's son, Prince Ajátasattu, to lead a coup d'état to take over the throne and the kingdom. That plan, if carried out properly, would bring about two results. The Buddha's main supporter would be eliminated, and Devadatta would ascend to the position of the new king's great master!

With this destructive plan in his head, Devadatta approached Prince Ajátasattu, showing him some magical, charismatic faith objects. The young Prince became confident and bestowed his trust in Devadatta, and the two became close friends. Prince Ajátasattu did not have the blood of a rebellious tyrant before, but because of his association with Devadatta, Ajátasattu lost himself in this pitfall.

The ambitious, foolish, and deluded Ajátasattu believed in his new master totally, and he arrested his father, King Bimbisára, putting him in jail without permission to receive visitors, even the King's own mother, and without any communication whatsoever. Ajátasattu cut off the king's food and water, and so tormented his own father, who had no way of fighting back. Despite the lamentations of his mother, Kosala Devi, and repeated requests to release his father, Devadatta paid no attention, until eventually King Bimbisára died in prison.

The unfortunate young prince, Ajátasattu, had become a cruel tyrant because of the monk Devadatta. After his success persuading Ajátasattu to revolt against his father, Devadatta was given the position of the new King's master and counsellor, overseeing all important things at the King's court. The first demand that Devadatta made of King Ajátasattu was the destruction of the Buddha, in order that Devadatta could establish himself as the leader of the Buddhist Sangha and thus of Buddhism as a whole.

Devadatta chose the worst destructive strategy. He ordered a group of the best archers to find the Buddha alone in an isolated place, while he was resting, and shoot him. But in the end, Devadatta was disappointed. His assassins changed their minds, for although they had killed many other people before, they could not find it in their hearts to murder the innocent Buddha. The Buddha did no wrong, but only performed all good things for humankind without any discrimination.

So the bowmen did not notch their arrows, but instead adopted the position of prayer. They bowed their heads and paid high respect, rather than lowering them to hide their criminal intention. The archers all laid down their arrows, and humbly requested the Buddha to deliver to them a discourse on the Dharma, which he did out of compassion for them. As a matter of fact, not only common people knew of the Buddha and appreciated his work, but also even many forest gangs and hoodlums admired his selfless service in helping and redeeming the people of all walks of life.

After this disappointment, Devadatta did not give up his attempts to destroy the Buddha. Instead, he made another plan to kill the Buddha openly. At that time, Devadatta was in the position to do anything he wanted, because he had King Ajâtasattu's total support and approval. Nonetheless, Devadatta realized that using human beings to kill a human being was unreliable, because they could change their mind, just as the archers had.

Now at the court of King Ajátasattu, there was an executing elephant, Nâlâgiri by name. This elephant was extremely cruel and drank a dozen of bottles of whisky daily. Devadatta decided to dispatch the elephant to kill the Buddha when the Buddha was making his rounds for morning alms.

News of this plot spread throughout Rájagaha, which caused great worry and concern among the lay Buddhists. Even so, the Buddha went out for morning alms as usual. That particular day, Devadatta fed the elephant a double quantity of whisky, and he sent the elephant directly against the Buddha, who was walking around in front of thousands and thousands of his lay followers. The elephant ran at high speed toward the Buddha, but then instead of killing him, Nâlâgiri stopped suddenly and bowed his head down toward his feet in a respectful manner, because of the loving-kindness (Mettâ) and compassion emanated by the Buddha. As a result, Nâlâgiri became as tame as a pet, and bent his head and tusks to the ground beside the Buddha's feet.

So, Devadatta lost his faith in human beings, and in animals, to accomplish his evil plans. Devadatta then decided to do the destructive deed himself, but he chose a very foolish means. He climbed to the top of a mountain and hid himself in the bushes not far from the ravine through which the Buddha would pass on his way down from Mount Gijjhakûta (Vulture's Peak). Devadatta waited impatiently until the Buddha arrived, and then Devadatta took a great rock and hurled it at the Buddha, intending to strike a fatal blow.

But Devadatta's intention to kill the Buddha became intolerable to the Heavenly Beings, and they therefore diverted that huge rock away from the Great Master of the world. The rock spirit refused to be used by the evil-minded Devadatta, and so rolled down and hit another rock on its way, breaking into small and large pieces. Only one little piece of the stone managed to hit the Buddha's foot. Once again, Devadatta had failed.

After this, Devadatta ran out of ideas for any further plans to destroy the Buddha. The Buddha, who had never had a bad thought about, nor expressed any hostile gesture toward, Devadatta, continued on his glorious path, gaining higher and wider respect from both his followers and from those who simply knew about him. In addition, those who might have been interested in joining with Devadatta turned away and became friends of the Buddha's disciples. This gave the Buddha more eyes and ears to track Devadatta's movements, plots and plans.

For this reason, Devadatta gave up assassination plans and began to think of political tricks that could be used to eliminate the Buddha. Devadatta gathered a group of monks who were new to the Dharma and the monastic disciplines. These new monks had just recently retired from the world, and they possessed very little intelligence. Devadatta convinced them to question the Buddha's authority, and enlisted them to dismantle Buddha's leadership, so that Devadatta could take over.

Devadatta proposed to the Buddha, as if he were handing the Buddha an ultimatum, recommendations for Five Points -- compulsory regulations that included rules prohibiting monks from eating meat and other restrictions. But the Buddha refused all these proposals, because they were only Devadatta's personal notions and were not practicable in any way. After learning of Buddha's refusal, Devadatta then asked the Buddha directly to turn over all authority to Devadatta. The Buddha, according to Devadatta, was getting old and should retire from administrative work, allowing Devadatta to perform for him the executive function of the Sangha. Once again, the Buddha refused this request.

Now, Devadatta became furious. He announced then and there that from that moment on he would not be subject to the Buddha and to the Sangha at large. He would establish a new sect and would become its only leader. So saying, Devadatta took those monks who would follow him and walked away from the well-established tradition led by the Great Master. Devadatta created a schism in the Sangha, and settled down with his followers at the foot of a mountain not too far from the Buddha's monastery.

At that time, the Venerable Moggallána, a chief disciple and the "left-hand" of the Buddha (Sáriputta was the Buddha's "right-hand"), knew about the tragedy and felt such great compassion for those monks who followed Devadatta that he took the trouble to go and point out to them what was right about the fundamental Buddhist practice. The majority of the monks, after learning the truth concerning the Buddha-Dharma through the clear explanation of Moggallána, returned to the Buddha's establishment. Only just a few monks were left with Devadatta.

All these things made Devadatta feel so deeply sorrowful and worried that he fell ill -- vomiting blood and laying down in the cave, as if he were totally abandoned and without any refuge. Thus the lives of those who committed bad actions against the innocent would have ended in this manner.

Nonetheless, the opportunity to change one's mind is always provided, and is made available to all at any moment by the natural, free flow of life. As for Devadatta, his illness became increasingly severe as the days passed. His physical body barely had any energy or vitality left, and his mind that used to be powerfully driven by heavy contaminations, calmed down enough that he could become aware of his offences. When he grew close to death, he asked his monks to carry him on a bed to the Buddha's residence -- in the hope that Devadatta might see the Buddha before death.

But it was too late. Devadatta's final breath took place during the trip, just before his arrival at the monastery where the Buddha was residing. Devadatta's devotional monks, who were now few in number, buried his dead body right there, at the very place where he had died. Devadatta's body was covered by the earth. Buddhist commentators viewed his body as being swallowed up and devoured by the planet Earth, so that he missed seeing the Buddha altogether.

From his residence, the Buddha made an announcement that he always had as much love, compassion and goodwill for

Devadatta and for the murderous bowmen, as he did for his own son, Râhula. The Buddha also said that Devadatta's consciousness was redirected to the right course at the last moment just before he died. Just as his path was crooked at the beginning, it became straight at the end. The Buddha predicted that Devadatta would be able to realize Nirvana and to become fully enlightened in a future life. Devadatta was swallowed up by the earth in that particular life because of the consequence of his grave karma committed against the Buddha, which no one could ever help him to avoid.

Mudra 56

Mudra 56

Mudra of Converting Baka, the Brahma

In this Mudra, the Buddha was in his standing posture with his eyes cast down, both of his hands lying gently on top of each other, that is to say, the right hand rested on top of the left hand, which was a gesture of mindful walking on the Brahma Baka's head.

The Buddha image of this mudra was carefully and prudently built by constructing it in form of the Brahma Baka with eight hands, all holding weapons, astride a particular bull Usabha [43] in a threatening manner, meanwhile having the Buddha stand on his (Brahma Baka's) head.

Illustrating Story:

There was a Brahma named Baka, who resided in a mythological Brahma world for a very long time. The time was so far beyond any ordinary measure of time that Baka wrongly and perniciously held the view that *all things without exception are permanent and without any change whatsoever. Everything remains what it is everlastingly, and no one can make any alterations to it.* This kind of perverted, wrong view is technically known as *sassaditthi, or eternalism.* Such a view existed long before the emergence of the Buddha. *Sassaditthi* is the opposite of another wrong view known as *ucchedaditthi*, or *nihilism*, which views all things and everything without exception as nihilistic.

Those maintaining such wrong views find it extremely difficult to understand the three characteristics of existence:

---

[43] A bull referring to manliness and strength, for example, a bull of a man, a very strong man.

impermanence, dissatisfaction, and void or lack of substance and permanent entity, let alone the realization of Truth. Baka Brahma, under the unyielding grip of such a pernicious, wrong view may be compared to an individual whose hand has been bitten by a poisonous snake. Certainly, such individual needs an immediate, urgent remedy; otherwise he will lose his life.

Therefore, the Buddha went to explain Dharma, the Truth, to Baka the Brahma, so that Baka would give up his pernicious, wrong view.

It took the Buddha quite a long while to convince the Brahma of the truth of the matter. Nonetheless, the Buddha transformed Baka with the sovereign remedy of Great Insight. The Great Insight is at the core of the Buddha's middle path as regards right view[44], which is summarized in four lines as follows:

> *When this is, that is.*
> *When this arises, that arises.*
> *When this is not, that is not.*
> *When this ceases, that ceases.*

Baka Brahma at first challenged the Buddha regarding the demonstration of some supernatural power, in this case, the issue of *disappearance*, which the Blessed Master accepted. Whenever and wherever the Brahma vanished, the Buddha

---

[44] In Pali: sammâ ditthi, which, in the practical sense of experiential realization, refers to the Perfect Insight-Knowledge of Four Noble Truths, namely, Dukkha (Dissatisfaction/Suffering), Arising of Dukkha (Craving/Thirst rooted in Ignorance or Lack of Inner Knowing), Cessation of Dukkha (Nirvana), and the Middle Path (Eightfold Path), which leads to the cessation of Dukkha. But in the philosophical sense it signifies the view between those two extreme views inflexibly grasped and maintained long before the emergence of the Buddha.

easily found him. In turn, when the Buddha made himself disappear, the Brahma attempted to search by all means, but totally failed to find the Buddha anywhere. Finally, Baka gave in and surrendered. And then the Buddha appeared and came out directly from Baka's own hair! That's how the story ended.

This story leads us to ask a number of questions. What kind of being is a Brahma? What kind of world does a Brahma inhabit? And what is meant by "the Buddha came out of the Brahma's hair"?

Mythologically, Brahma is a highly developed being living in a higher plane of life called the "brahma-loka", the world of Brahma, which existed somewhere in the mythological realm. Some Buddhists and some Hindus believe in such a realm. But you don't have to believe or disbelieve, since it's your freedom to choose. My own view is that Brahma represents a human being who achieves one of the various stages of jhâna (meditative absorption) through his or her meditational development and spiritual growth. Hence, Baka the Brahma refers to an individual who has accomplished the second stage of "jhâna with form" (rûpa-jhâna), since he is of great purity, radiant light, and psychic power. He belongs to the category of "âbhassara-brahma", the brahma of exceedingly bright light, as discussed below.

Let me share some details concerning the variety of brahmas in accordance with the Buddhist text and my own experiential realization.

Those beings that reside in this level of altered states of consciousness, technically known as Jhânic Consciousness (Jhâna-citta), earn the denomination of "brahma", as they have achieved the various stages of the meditative absorption (Jhâna), and these are divided into sixteen grades, in accordance with the four stages of Jhâna with Form (rûpa jhána) as follows:

1. The plane of the First Jhâna comprises three grades of brahma, namely:
   a) The realm of the retinue of brahma (brahma parisajjâ)
   b) The realm of the brahma ministers (brahma purohita)
   c) The realm of the great brahma (mahâbrahma).
2. The plane of the second jhâna also comprises three grades of brahma:
   a) The realm of minor radiance (partitâbhâ)
   b) The realm of infinite radiance (appamânâbhâ)
   c) The realm of the radiantly shining brahma (âbhassara brahma). It is said that the rays of light are evidently radiated out of those radiant brahmas' bodies as quickly as flashes of lightening.
3. The plane of the third jhâna consists of three grades as follows:
   a) The realm of the brahmas with minor aura (parittasubhâ)
   b) The realm of the brahmas with infinite aura (appamânasubhâ)
   c) The realm of the brahmas with serene aura (subhakinha, lit. good light, which means the mass of serene light radiates out of their bodies).
4. The plane of the fourth jhâna consists of three grades as follows:
   a) The realm of the brahmas with great reward (vehapphala – abundant reward as the result of the jhâna practice).
   b) The realm of the brahmas without ideation (asaññâsatta)

c) The realm of the brahmas in the pure abode (suddhâvâsa), which is subdivided in five categories, namely:
a) The durable realm (avihâ)
b) The serene realm (atappâ)
c) The beautiful realm (sudassâ)
d) The realm of clear vision (sudassî)
e) The highest realm where the supreme beings dwell (akanittha)

The Rest of the Story

Converting Baka, the Brahma, of the Pernicious, Wrong View and of Self-Deception into the Noble Middle Path.

Individuals who practice the method of *calm and concentrated meditation* technically known as *samatha*, and have reached a stage of jhâna, will naturally earn the title of "brahma". Hence, the symbolic Baka, the Brahma, was one of these individuals who accomplished the second stage of the absorptive jhânic meditation, and further methodically developed supernatural power until he had achieved it satisfactorily. But the *inner meaning* of Baka, the Brahma, here refers to holding a pernicious, wrong view, together with self-deception, as described in the story.

The Dharma Weapon used by the Buddha was *Great Insight* into what the *Truth* really is. This led Baka to abandon his pernicious, wrong view, to relinquish his distorted truths, and to stop deceiving himself altogether. Baka then adopted and followed the Buddha's middle path[45].

---

[45] This path consists of eight factors, namely, Right Understanding (balanced view), Right Thought (thinking with the heart), Right Action, Right Speech, Right

The specific practice leading to gaining the Great Insight is the mindfulness path of Insight Meditation. The concise description of this practice, together with some concrete instructions for carrying out Insight Meditation, has been provided in the last section of Triumph #6[46].

Nonetheless, the author would like to make a brief comment on the accomplishment of jhâna or meditative absorption done without an absolutely essential supportive system for gaining Penetrative Insight and Inner Wisdom. It is extremely dangerous to follow exclusively the samatha system of calm and exceedingly concentrated meditation[47], and then develop solely the definitive method for achieving psychic, supernatural power. Power without wisdom and love is conducive to destruction, cruelty, and brutality. At the personal growth level, psychic, spiritual power without the unsurpassed light of wisdom to guide the way of life and to help carry out the spiritual activity will impede further growth, put the maturity on hold, damage the soul, and destroy the capacity to see things as they are (to directly know the Truth as is really is). In addition, an extreme, pernicious, wrong view can set in, putting the individual holding such a view into an inescapable trap. So, the most effective remedy is the

---

Livelihood, Right Perseverance, Right (impeccable) Mindfulness, and Right Samadhi.

[46] See details in same author's book in its Spanish version entitled *Los Gloriosos Triunfos del Buda*, privately published by the author on his 80th Birthday commemoration, 2014.

[47] See a concise description of this practice in the same author's book *The Way of Non-Attachment* (INTRODUCTION), which is also available in French and in Spanish.

practice of Vipassana Insight Meditation[48], together with the Buddha's Middle Path[49].

---

[48]See a detailed description of the Vipassana Practice in the same author's book entitled *Vipassana and Gestalt Therapy*. Also, in Spanish as *Meditación Vipassana y Gestalt* published by Mandala Editiones, 2008.

[49]See some details in *Una Nueva Visión del Budismo* by the same author, published by Ediciones La Llave, 2004.

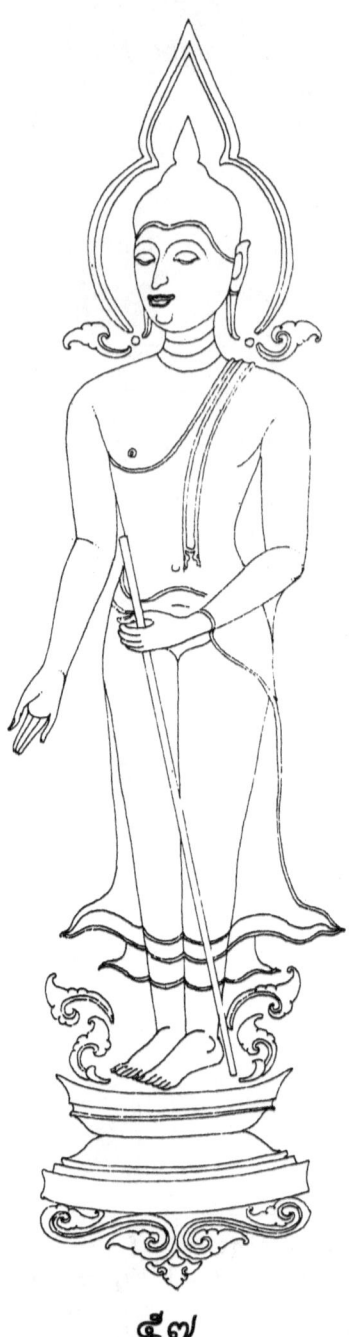

Mudra 57

Mudra 57

Mudra of Contemplating Loathsomeness/Impurity

In this mudra the Buddha was in his standing posture, and it exists in two styles: One style having his left hand hang down and rested on his left thigh while his right hand stretches outward in the manner of pulling a cloth. In another style, his left hand holds a staff while the right hand was held in the same position as that of the first style.

Illustrating Story:

At one time the Buddha was residing in Uruvela, Kassapa's ashram, where he lived together with his jatila disciples, five hundred in number, for the sole purpose of subduing and converting them to Dharma. At that time, Punnadâsi, a female servant of a millionaire in Râjagaha city, died, and her master let other servants of his wrap up her corpse with a white, clean cloth, and then carry it to a woods cemetery as popularly practiced in those days. When the Buddha who needed such a white cloth for making an outer rope for himself, knew of the occurrence, he went there alone.

At that time, Punnadâsi's corpse became quite decomposed and swollen all over, from which yellow liquids flowed out and numerous worms ate it up. Upon his arrival the Buddha, while reflecting and meditating on loathsomeness, ugliness, and impurity of her corpse, began to pull out the white cloth from the corpse that remained in such an appalling condition. In his manner of pulling, he first shook off all the worms gently and then dragged it out mindfully, and immediately afterward carried that dirty, white cloth with him on the way back to his residence.

Right away, the Buddha washed it, dried it in the sun, and then folded it up nicely after it had been dry, of course, and all this was done by himself (with a great help from Indra, King of Távatimsa heaven, mythologically speaking). Soon after that, he cut the cloth into different pieces, sewed them all together, dyed the product in a saffron color.He then made it his outer robe (similar to an overcoat) and used it for quite a long time in a cold temperature or at night when the weather turned chilly.

Sometimes later, he encountered an old monk, Elder Maha Kassapa, whose outer rope was rather overweight and quite heavy to carry around, so the Buddha offered to him his new outer rope for which the former appreciated deeply the Buddha's empathy and great compassion. The Buddha said to Maha Kassapa thus: *Oh, Kassapa! Your outer rope made of a gross material was quite thick and heavy, let us exchange with mine, which was incredibly refined and more comfortable, so that it could be much lighter and more convenient for carrying with you when moving about in your wandering life. Responding gratefully to the Great Master's kind offer, Maha Kassapa accepted it with his deep thankfulness and great joy.*

Mudra 58

Mudra 58

Mudra of Reflecting on the Nature of Decay

In this mudra the Buddha was seated in the samadhi posture with both of his hands covering and resting over his knees.

Illustrating Story:

Since his attainment of complete enlightenment and delivery of the first sermon called *turning the irreversible wheel of Dharma* to the five ascetics at the deer sanctuary in Benares, and at the end of which one of them, Kondañña, attained to initial but irreversible enlightenment and became the first monk in the Buddha's Monastic Order, the Buddha continued giving discourses on the dharma, spreading his teachings near and far until Buddhasâsana (Dharma and Vinaya) was successfully and firmly established in Magadha Super Power State. And then he carried out his Dharma Mission, helping countless men and women reach enlightenment, accomplish immeasurable freedom through putting an end of suffering once and for all, and realize nirvana, the ultimate truth and complete cessation of internal fires of all kinds, be they emotional, mental, psychological, or spiritual. Such a selfless and tireless mission was notably successful and exceedingly beneficial to people of all walks of life during his forty-five years of rendering it.

Entering the forty-fifth year, the final year of his mission, the Buddha resided in a village named veluvagâma in the territory of Vesâli, the capital city of Vajjî, another Super Power State. At that time he got severely ill, bearing a great deal of almost unbearable physical pains through pure mindfulness and clear comprehension, or sati-sampajañña, until eventually all those pains diminished without troubling him mentally and emotionally. The other dharmas he used for dealing with the acute pains were: *durable patience, invincible perseverance in removing the disease and healing the illness, and insight into the nature of pain as merely an unpleasant sensation.* After all pains had gone, one day he seated himself on a seat prepared for him under the shadow of the vihâra; then, Ananda, his attendant monk, entered to pay his proper respect and to render his services to the Great Master[50].

Then and there the Buddha spoke to him (Ananda) about the nature of decay as follows:

Ananda! Now I am eighty years old, of an advanced age. Tathâgata's physical body is quite weak and with much less strength, just like an old tree on the edge of a river. Oh! Ananda! Any time Tathâgata[51] meditates and enters **rapture of mind** *through* **ceto samadhi,** *samadhi without signs or images while the mind is firmly and unwaveringly stabilized in which uncomfortable and disagreeable feelings or sensations cease to exist but the samadhi free from any signs or mental pictures whatsoever prevails. In such a meditative state, Tathâgata's body is indeed radiant, exceptionally fine, and fully at ease.*

Ananda! This animitasamâdhi-dharma (samadhi without images or signs) has so much power that it can make its practitioner happy, peaceful, and blissful. Therefore, you and other follow monks should take refuge in **Self** *and not in any other thing or person, that is to say, you all must take Dharma as your* **island** *and your* **refuge** *in every and all postures.* Thus saying, the Great Master continued expounding the subject of **having self as refuge**, which refers to the practice of satipatthâna-bhâvanâ[52],

---

[50] In Pali, parama satthâ.
[51] That was how the Buddha referred to himself instead of using the word "I".
[52] Vipassana Meditation founded in Mindfulness as regards the body, feeling/sensation, mind and mental sates, and intellectual and spiritual subjects of the dharmâ.

the unique, irreplaceable path to immeasurable emancipation and full enlightenment.

The Buddha proceeded with carrying out his dharma mission at the Veluvagâma village throughout the winter season (approximately three months).

Mudra 59

Mudra 59

Mudra of Presenting A Copious Portent

In this mudra the Buddha was seated in the samadhi[53] posture with his left hand raised to his chest level while his right hand rested on his right knee.

Illustrating Story:

The story relating to this mudra is included the mudra of announcing his forthcoming death, mudra number 61, with its full illustrating story.

---

[53] Samâdhi would comprise (a) the guarding of senses, (b) impeccable awareness and self-recollection, (c) inner contentment, (d) emancipation from hindrances, and (e) meditative absorption or jhâna.

Mudra 60

Mudra 60

Mudra of Prohibiting Mâra

In this mudra, the Buddha was seated in the samadhi posture with his left hand gently placed on his lap, palm facing upwards, while his right hand with its open palm was raised to his chest level and facing forward, away from his body, indicating the gesture of prohibition.

Illustrating Story:

The related story of this mudra is included in that of announcing his forthcoming death, which is mudra number 61. Let us read it carefully in the following pages.

Mudra 61

Mudra 61

Mudra of Announcing His Forthcoming Death

In this mudra the Buddha was seated in the samadhi posture, with his left hand gently placed on his left knee while his right hand with its open palm was raised and turned toward his chest in a comportment of stroking the body.

Illustrating Story:

In the morning of full moon day of March the Buddha picked his alms-bowl and entered Vesâli city for collecting alms-food, and after returning to the monastery and having a good meal he asked Ananda to carry his seat-cloth to set up a seat for him at Pâvâla Cetiya so that he could relax and rest during the daytime, which he did, while Ananda took his own seat nearby. At that time the Buddha wished that Ananda would respectfully ask him to live for one hundred years or more, so he presented Ananda with a copious portent by pointing out clearly that meditation on the *four bases of wonder* or iddhi[54], namely, *the establishing of determination concerning concentration on purpose, on will, mobilization of energy, concentration on thought*

---

[54] Iddhi (potency) in pre-Buddhistic time refers to the four wonders of a king, namely, personal beauty, long life, good health, and popularity while the iddhi of a rich young noble is (1) the use of beautiful garden, (2) the use of soft and pleasant clothes, (3) the use of different houses for the different seasons, (4) consumption of good food (healthy diet). Concerning the Buddhist theory of iddhi, the Buddha was represented as saying "It is because I see the danger in the practice of these mystic wonders that I loathe and abhor and am ashamed thereof". The mystic wonder that he himself believed in and dedicated humslf to was the wonder of education. What education was meant in the case of iddhi we learn from the four bases of psychic power (iddhi), as given in the *Pali-English Dictionary of Pali Text Society*, 2004, as found in the above-quoted text.

or silent contemplation (inner thinking or thinking from the heart), and concentration on investigation or exertion (the use of mega power) of penetrating wisdom.

He repeated to Ananda three times the benefit of practicing the iddhipâda meditation through which its practitioner would be able to live for one kappa (one hundred years) or more. But, because Mâra possessed his mind and prevented him from comprehending the clue, Ananda failed to make such a request. Then the Buddha told him to leave him alone, and he did accordingly.

Soon after Ananda left, Mâra approached the Buddha, reminding him of what he said after his full enlightenment during his stay under the ajapâla-nigrodha tree thus: *"So long as his fourfold parisâ, namely, bhikkhu parisâ, bhikkhuni parisâ, upâsaka parisâ, and upâsikâ parisâ, were not wise enough nor did spread widely the practice of noble and propitious life for the welfare, for the benefit, and for the happiness of the many, he would not enter parinirvana (final death)."* Mâra further told the Buddha that now all those objectives that were to be achieved had been accomplished, and it therefore was an appropriate time for him to pass away for good.

After Mâra had thus said, the Buddha prohibited him in his roaring voice as follows: *"Oh, Mâra, Evil One! Make no effort in persuading Tathâgata with respect to his parinirvana, he would enter into it within three months from now on.*

Soon after the Great Master of the world had announced his forthcoming death or parinirvana (utter cessation without remainder) with pure mindfulness and totally clear comprehension at the Pâvâla Cetiya, the entire earth trembled, and divine drums sounded throughout the whole sky. Encountering such a wonder, Ananda immediately abandoned his resting place under a big tree nearby and approached the

Buddha, asking him about the causes of various wonders that took place, which the Great Master revealed in these words:

*"Ananda! The causes of the earth treble are eight, they are: (1) severe turbulence and upheaval of wind or the sudden and violent changes in the direction that air or water is moving in or the forceful motions of the earth hitting each other suddenly and violently, (2) psychic power of the person endowed with iddhi or siddhi, (3) a bodhisatva or Buddha-to.be descends in his mother's womb, (4) the birth of the bodhisattva, (5) a Tathâgata attains to complete enlightenment, (6) the Tathâgata delivers his first discourse on the **"irreversible motion of Dharma**", (7) the Tathâgata announces his forthcoming parinirvana or final death, and (8) the Tathâgata enters into parinirvana or cessation without remainder."*

Then he made it clear to Ananda that he had announced his forthcoming death, and for that reason the earth trembled all over the planet. Upon hearing such a sad statement from the Great Master, Ananda immediately requested him to live for one kappa for the welfare, for the benefit, and for the happiness of the many in those are included devas, brahmas, and human beings. To his undue petition, the Buddha told Ananda that it was too late since he did not make his request at the time when Tathâgata related to him the meditation on fourfold iddhipâda that caused its practitioner to live for a minimum of one kappa. If Ananda would have made his petition at that time, then the Buddha could have lived for a hundred years or more.

In order to lessen Ananda's severe sadness and overwhelming remorse, the Buddha made to him the following remarks: *"Ananda! Tathâgata has repeatedly said that all beings with no exception would be deprived of the loved ones since all the conditioned, made-up, created things are impermanent, subjected to change, and do not last forever, and therefore it's not worth attempting to derive one's durable satisfaction, everlasting gratification, and permanent pleasure from such unendurable things and/or living beings that only exist temporarily. Whatever arises depending upon the other thing(s), will sooner or later be broken up and eventually vanish from existence. Ananda! Do not lament about or want that which has the nature of arising and passing away momentarily, or lasting or continuing to exist for a long, long time. Ananda! Whatever Tathâgata has relinquished, died from, utterly let go of, and become definitively non-attached to, he will never bring back to life such unendurable, constantly changeable, and (by their very nature) dissatisfactory things. Therefore, Tathâgata will definitely pass away within three months, that is to say, on full moon day of May*[55] *(three months after his death-announcement).*

---

[55] The announcement was made on the full moon day of March.

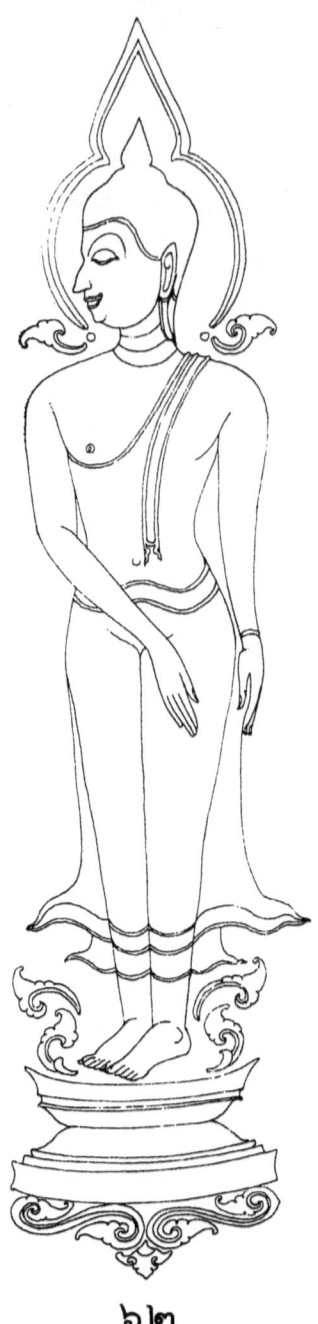

Mudra 62

Mudra 62

Mudra of Elephant-Look[56] (turning the whole body)

In this mudra the Buddha was in his standing posture with his right hand hanging down and stretched across his body to touch his left thigh, while his right hand was stretching downward alongside his body in the normal fashion; his face was turned toward his right shoulder, looking backward. This implies his final momentary look at Vesâli city in a way of saying "good-bye" to it since he will not be able to return to such a rich, beautiful, and resourceful city anymore.

Illustrating Story:

At one time, the Buddha accompanied by five hundred monks went to Vesâli and stayed at kûtâgâra hall. At that time the Licchavi monarchs, knowing of his arrival and of his taking residence there, were exceedingly pleased and happy, so they all went to have their audiences with him and presented numerous offerings to him. Then and there the Blessed One delivered to them a distinguished discourse appropriate to the occasion, encouraging them to continue upholding faith and taking delight in the dharma. At the end of his discourse, those Licchavi monarchs extended their invitation to him and to all of his monks for having meals at their grand palace, and then they took leave of him.

The following morning the Buddha together with his numerous monks went to take their meals at the grand palace. After the meal he once again gave another suitable dharma talk to those righteous monarchs, and then left them for his

---

[56] In Pali, nâgâvalokita, which is a mark of the Buddhas since an elephant is gifted with miraculous powers and great strength, as is a Buddha.

residence. But at the moment of his arrival at the city gate, the Buddha turned his face toward the great city of Vesâli as if he were fond of it with all his heart, and said to Ananda thus: "*Ananda! This look at Vesâli of Tathâgata is the final one.*" Then he continued walking toward the kûtâgâra residence located in the immense forest and remained there for a considerable period of time.

The place where the Buddha stood and demonstrated his elephant-look at Vesâli turned out to be a significant Cetiya popularly known as "*nâgâvalokita cetiya*". Here are some reasons for the significance of his elephant-look that caused the people to have a cetiya built for marking it:

1. Vesâli was a large city where a great number of the Buddha's fourfold parisâ lived, and he himself paid numerous visits there with his attempts to get his Sâsana (Dharma and Vinaya) securely established. So, his final look at the significant city of Vesâli in the manner of elephant-look indicated that he would not return to it anymore. Nonetheless, such a gesture of looking marked an important reminder to those great people of Vesâli, both Buddhists and non-Buddhists alike, of the Great Master's multiple visits as well as of his Dharma and Vinaya firmly rooted in the hearts and minds of many citizens of Vesâli.
2. Also, the Buddha's elephant-look at such an important city implied a portent that he would enter into his final passing away (parinirvana) some time soon after his departure from Vesâli, which was quite true to the historical fact.
3. Vesâli was the massive and sovereign city of Vajjî Super Power State ruled by the United Licchavi Monarchs who governed the city and its State by

following strictly the leaders' dharmic virtues [57] imparted to them by the Buddha, and guiding their people with mettâ (universal and boundless love), compassion, and wisdom. The specific dharma that the Buddha gave to the Licchavi monarchs is technically called "licchavi-aparihâniya-dharma – conditions leading to prosperity and glory" in which he laid a strong emphasis on *unity, democracy, reconciliation, and constant counseling with one another.* In brief, he urged them to rule in righteousness, not shaking up the tenfold code of the king, monarch, or leader (dasa râjadhammâ) as written (in the footnote below). For that very reason, Vesâli maintained its sovereignty, prosperity, and freedom.

---

[57] They are alms giving and generosity, ethical conduct or morality, liberality or benevolence, straightness or rectitude, gentleness, self-control, non-anger, non-hurtfulness or non-violence, forbearance or patience, and non-obstructiveness (not making himself a problem or an obstacle but being part of solution).

Mudra 63

Mudra 63

Mudra of Receiving Drinking Water

In this mudra the Buddha was seated in the samadhi posture with his open left hand rested on his lap while his right hand was holding his alms-bowl and placed on his right knee, indicating the act of receiving drinking water.

Illustrating Story:

At the time of his stay at Pâvâla Cetiya in the vicinity of Vesâli the Buddha gave distinctive instructions to his monks on taking Dharma as their refuge. Soon after that he left for bhandugâma accompanied by them, residing leisurely in that village and delivering some distinguished discourses on the dharma to the fourfold assemblies (parisâ), namely, bhikkhus, bhikkhunis, upâsakas, and upâsikâs, up to the point that they all became firmly established in the dharmas (conditions) leading to freedom from all contaminations and intoxications. Those dharmas were ethical conduct or code of discipline (sîla), firmly stabilized mind (samâdhi), wisdom (paññâ), and emancipation or liberation from dukkha (vimutti).

Some time after that he together with his monks traveled to various villages such as Hatthigâma, Ambugâma, Jambugâma, and Bhoga-nagara, and took residence in the last of these, delivering discourses on the suitable dharma to the citizens of that city, and then moved on to Pâvâ-nagara and stayed in the mango grove prepared for him and his following monks by Cunda Kammâraputta, the owner of that delightful and beautiful garden. There he gave an appropriate dharma talk to Cunda so that the latter attained to the initial but irreversible enlightenment, or the fruition of entry in the eternal flow of nirvana. Before taking leave of the Buddha, Cunda then invited him and his monks to have a meal at his mansion in the city, which the Great Master accepted in serene silence.

During the evening and night of that particular day, Cunda together with his wife and servants were preparing a variety of food, including a delicious, soft (tender) boar's flesh[58]. The following morning the Buddha accompanied by a great number of his monks went to his residence for their brunch (breakfast and lunch combined). Since the Buddha knew that there was some poison in that tender boar's meat prepared over night, he told Cunda not to offer it to any other monks but to him only, and that the remaining tender boar's meat was to be buried in the ground; the latter did accordingly. After the meal, as always, the Blessed One gave a suitable dharma talk for thanking and expressing his appreciation so that the donor and his party reached a great joy and stabilized their unwavering faith in Tiratana: Buddha, Dharma, and Sangha, and then he returned to the mango grove with all his monks.

On that very day, he got sick with vomiting up some blood and tolerated an acute stomach pain. therefore told Ananda to prepare a journey to Kusinârâ, and the latter did so in accordance with his wish by announcing the trip to all the resident monks so that they could get ready to accompany the Great Master.

Along the way the Buddha was attempting to heal his illness by applying a specific sweet medicine called "overpowering attainment[59] meditation", in which he entered into an unsurpassed, fathomlessly deep samâdhi, the samâdhi devoid of images and prevailing in an eternal void. At a certain point of the travel, the Blessed One became thirsty and therefore

---

[58] Sûkaramaddava.
[59] Samâpatti-bhâvanâ specifically referring to saññâ-vedayita-norodha samâpatti, the attainment acquired by the Buddha in which perception and sensation utterly cease.

told Ananda to look for some drinking water to quench his thirst. Since he found only a muddy water unsuitable for drinking, Ananda came back to report it to the Great Master who, in turn, insisted that he would find it. Once again, Ananda went out in search for drinking water, thinking that the Buddha might have seen it somewhere through his insightful, visionary eye, which was true that he eventually found that miraculous water which was crystal clear, cool, and clean perfectly suitable for drinking, and then brought it to him.

It was the first and only time during the trip that the Buddha was thirsty and asked for drinking water. The reason for that lies in the actual fact that he was extremely ill and the end of his life was approaching him. So he made the following remark: *"Sankkhâras (conditioned, made-up or constructed, things) are indeed Mâra[60] that destroy peace and happiness, no matter if they belong to any beings; there is no exception, even Tathâgata is included."*

---

[60] Khandha-Mâra.

Mudra 64

Mudra 64

Mudra of Prediction

In this mudra the Buddha was in his reclining posture in which he lay down on his right side with his head resting on the pillow while his left hand was lying alongside his body and his right hand gently placed on his belly. This posture is technically known as "lion-lying position – sihaseyyâ".

Illustrating Story:

On his way to Kusinârâ, the Buddha took a break and rested under a huge tree beside the road, drinking the water offered to him by Ananda for quenching his thirst, and relaxing. At that time a noble man, named Pukkusa, of the monarch Malla, who was a disciple of the Buddha's former master, Âlâla Kâlâma, was on a trip to Pâvâ-nagara. At a glance at the Great Master, he felt deeply moved and highly lifted, so he approached him and after paying his proper respects to him, sat down at a suitable place. Then the Blessed One imparted to him the dharma of "how to live in peace". After hearing that eloquent dharma talk, he became unwaveringly convinced of the Buddha-Dharma, and then offered him a pair of the incredibly neat, exclusively beautiful, and most valuable cloth of gold color known as *singi,* which the Great Master accepted out of compassion and empathy. Then he told Pukkusa to cover his physical body with one piece of that cloth and to give another piece to Ananda, which he did accordingly. As always the case, the Buddha gave him another eloquent dharma talk, and Pukkusa was then filled with a great joy and utter delight in the dharma, and took leave of the Blessed One, continuing his journey to his destination.

With his body dressed in the singi-vanna cloth, the indescribable radiance and utmost transparency of the Buddha's physical body shined forth so amazingly and miraculously that

Ananda became stunningly overwhelmed in witnessing this with his own eyes. He then made a comment on that unspeakable beauty which the Great Master shared with him, saying that there were only two occasions when his physical body became exceedingly radiant and thoroughly illuminating: First was when he attained to perfect enlightenment, and second was that time which was close to his parinirvana, which would take place that very night of full moon day in May, under the pair of Sala trees in the Sala forest that belonged to the Malla Monarch, Great King of Malla State. Having thus spoken, he asked Ananda to take him to Kakudhâ-nadî River for bathing himself and enjoying its fresh and clean water.

Soon after that, the Buddha left for the pair of Sala trees, and upon their arrival, he asked Ananda to lay down on the ground between the two Sala trees his outer robe or sanghâti on which he lay down his body comfortably, in the lion-position, of course. There he took a peaceful rest and relaxed his entire body, which endured a great deal of hardship during such a long trip.

After having had a good rest, the Buddha told Ananda that if anyone would blame Cunda for that last meal that he had prepared and offered to him, causing him parinirvana, Ananda and all the monks should settle the issue harmoniously and comprehensively as well as bring peace of mind to Cunda. That was because those two significant meals offered to Tathâgata on the most important occasions were exceedingly fruitful, utterly beneficial, and brought about a long, healthy, and happy life to the donors. They were the meal offered to him by Sujâta, the millionaire of Sâvatthi, which he had eaten and then reached full enlightenment, another was the meal offered to him by Cunda, the wealthy man of Kusinârâ, which after he had eaten, led him to enter into parinirvana (ultimate extinction with no remainder).

Having made such a statement the Buddha accompanied by Ananda and numerous monks continued his journey and crossed over the Hiraññavati River which ran through Kusinârâ city, and went into the large Sala Botanical Garden that belonged to the Malla Monarch and was located in the neighborhood of the said city. Then and there, he asked Ananda to prepare a death-bed for him at a site between the pair of Sala trees, and he then lay down on it in his lion- sleep position with mindfulness and clear comprehension (sati-sampajañña) firmly and totally established, and with no intention or consideration to rise from it as it would be his final lying down[61] on the planet Earth.

At that time, it was said that those two Sala trees burst out blossoming, and then their fresh flowers fell down smoothly and lovingly on his physical body in the gesture of paying the ultimate respect to the Buddha. In addition, the utmost beautiful flowers of mandâ in the heavenly planes of life fell down from the skies to show their greatest honor to him; not only that, even those devas (shining beings) in their heavens played their divine music for honoring the Tathâgata, which sent out the wonderful sounds and astonished vibrations throughout the whole universe.

Then, the Buddha said to Ananda as follows:

"Ananda! The act of worshipping Tathâgata with such abundant material things as these is not considered the true worship. Ananda! Whoever practices the dharma worth practicing and does it in the right way, will be taken into account the respectable practitioner who truly pays his/her greatest honor to the Tathâgata." He then turned his attention to those assemblies of bhikkhus, bhikkhunis, and lay devotees present at his near-death place, admonishing them for their steady and resolute practices of Dharma and Vinaya or teachings and disciplinary (ethical) code of conduct both for their own benefits individually

---

[61] In Pali, seyyâvasâna.

and collectively for the stability and prosperity of Buddhasâsana in order that all beings that walk, creep, crawl, and live on earth would derive a great advantage from it.

At that very moment, he ordered Upavâna Thera, who was standing and creating a wind for the Tathâgata's bodily coolness and pleasantness, to leave him alone. Ananda became rather concerned over the Great Master's action and therefore, thought to himself, "in fact, Upavâna was another attendant of his for quite a long time, why did the Buddha send him away?" So, he approached him and inquired into the matter concerned, to which the Great Master responded, "Oh, Ananda! At that particular moment all devas from their heavenly planes had arrived for paying their proper respect to Tathágata, and taking their final look at him, but Upavâna was obstructing their views by standing there. That was the reason for my commanding him to vacate the place."

To Ananda's concerns over informal opportunities for having a warm audience and conversing with him familiarly the Buddha said this to him, *"Ananda! As practiced before, after the Lent observance* (the three-month period for contemplation), *the parisâ of bhikkhus, bhikkhunis, upâsakas, and upâsikâs from various places and from all directions came to have their close visits with Tathâgata, but after his parinirvana they all can go for paying their visits to four memorable places connected to Tathâgata, namely,* **his birth place, the place where he reached Buddhahood, the place where he delivered the first sermon, and his death (parinirvana) place.** *Those four places are valuable, notable, and outstanding for the visits to be paid by the four parisâ (assemblies) of bhikkhus, bhikkhunis, upâsakas, and upâsikâs. By so doing, they could remember him, see him inwardly, and commemorate him personally as they deem fit."*

To the specific question posed by Ananda, he replied as follows: *"Ananda! Do not be too concerned about what to do with the Tathâgata's dead body, but attempt diligently and persevere inconvincibly to bring your personal growth and development to completion in order that the tremendously excellent life of sanctity and spirituality (Brahmacariya) can be satisfactorily fulfilled. As for my dead physical body, those monarchs, brahmanas, and wealthy people, who take refuge in Tathâgata would know for certain what should be done with it."*

Finally, the Buddha made this statement to Ananda, "*Ananda! You don't have to be sorrowful, do not have to lament over Tathâgata's passing away since all conditioned things (sankkhâras) are impermanent and subject to change. Ananda! All things without exception that have arisen or come into existence, will naturally go through changes during their growth processes, and eventually end in death."* After saying that the Great Master of the world made such a prediction as this to Ananda: "*Ananda! You are filled with merits accumulated not only in this life on earth but for many lifetimes. You are wise, and carry out your duty with good knowledge and keen wisdom. Just continue making further good attempt and persevere constantly, soon you will achieve the extinction of all contaminations, that is to say, to become fully enlightened before the commencing day of the first council for Sangîti or sangâyati (sangâyana, which refers to the general convocation of the Buddhist monks in order to settle questions of doctrine and to fix the text of the Scriptures. The first Council is taken by tradition to have been held three months after the Buddha's parinirvana (final death), at Rajagaha, the Capital City of Magadha State, or Bihar at the present time).*

Mudra 65

Mudra 65

Mudra of Admonishing Subhadda

In this mudra the Buddha was in his lying-on-the-right-side posture with his head on the pillow while his left hand stretched along the left side of his body and his right hand was raised with the fingers gesturing in a specific way that indicated the act of teaching.

Illustrating Story:

After he predicted Ananda's full enlightenment to be reached three months after his final passing away, the Buddha then rested peacefully on his deathbed. Then Ananda approached him and suggested that he should not enter into parinirvana in such a small city of Kusinara, but in one of the largest cities such as Rajagaha, or Sâvatthi, so that it would match with his supremacy of the Greatest Master of the world. Hearing that the Tathâgata made a comment as follows:

"Ananda! This Kusinara city in the far past was the greatest and largest city called Kusâvati, the resident city of a great emperor named Sudassa, the ruler of Malla State[62], with Kusâvati as its capital city (at present, Kasia, in Northern Nepal). Kusinara or Kusi-nagara was the resourceful city packed with all the things for supplying the human needs and desires for a happy, pleasurable, and heavenly life on earth, and its citizens lived in peace, in harmony, in prosperity, and in considerable freedom under the reign of Emperor Sudassa." After thus saying, the

---

[62] Malla State was situated next to Eastern Kosala Super Power State, to Northern Vajji Super Power State, and in the East of Sakyan or Sakka State. Its capital city was Kusi-Nagara or Kusinara, which was built at the merging site between the two rivers, namely, Rapti River and Gandhaka River, in the north of Nepal.

Buddha dispatched Ananda to Kusinara city to inform the Monarch of Malla State that Tathâgata would enter into parinirvana at the end of this full moon night under the pair of Sala trees in his most peaceful and lovely Botanical Garden. Hearing such a sad news, the Malla Monarch together with his Queen, royal families, and dignitaries immediately left for the Sala Garden to have their audiences with the Buddha, their Great Master, and Ananda managed super efficiently the way by which they all could get close to the Tathâgata, group after group, in order of importance and significance.

On that occasion, a paribbâjaka (wondering mendicant), Subhadda by name, who lived in Kusinara city, heard of the Buddha's parinirvana and thought to himself that he had several unresolved questions to ask the Great Master of the world. So, he hastily went to the Royal Botanical Garden of Sala Trees, and without delay spoke to Ananda, requesting that he allow him to approach and pay his respects to the Buddha and to ask him about a most doubtful matter that had been bothering him for quite a long time. While Ananda was talking to Subhadda saying that the Great Master was too ill to take any questions from anyone, the Buddha overheard their conversation, and then told Ananda to let Subhadda in. Needless to say how delighted and happy Subhadda was in receiving such compassion from the Great Master, and therefore he went in and presented his question about the most distinguished masters in those days, who claimed to be perfectly enlightened. His question was if it was true that they were as they claimed. Instead of responding to such a question in a personal way, the Buddha cut the questioning short and simply said to him thus: "Oh, Subhadda! Don't bother about those masters. Listen attentively to what Tathâgata would tell you. There is a unique, excellent path called the eightfold path, namely: Right Understanding, Right Thought, Right Speech, Right Action, Right Livelihood, Right Perseverance, Right Mindfulness, and Right Concentration (Samadhi) that leads its practitioner to complete enlightenment. This path exists only in *the Buddha's Dharma and Vinaya, and not anywhere else. So long as the practice of the eightfold path is carried out genuinely and authentically, the world is never devoid of Arahatta."*

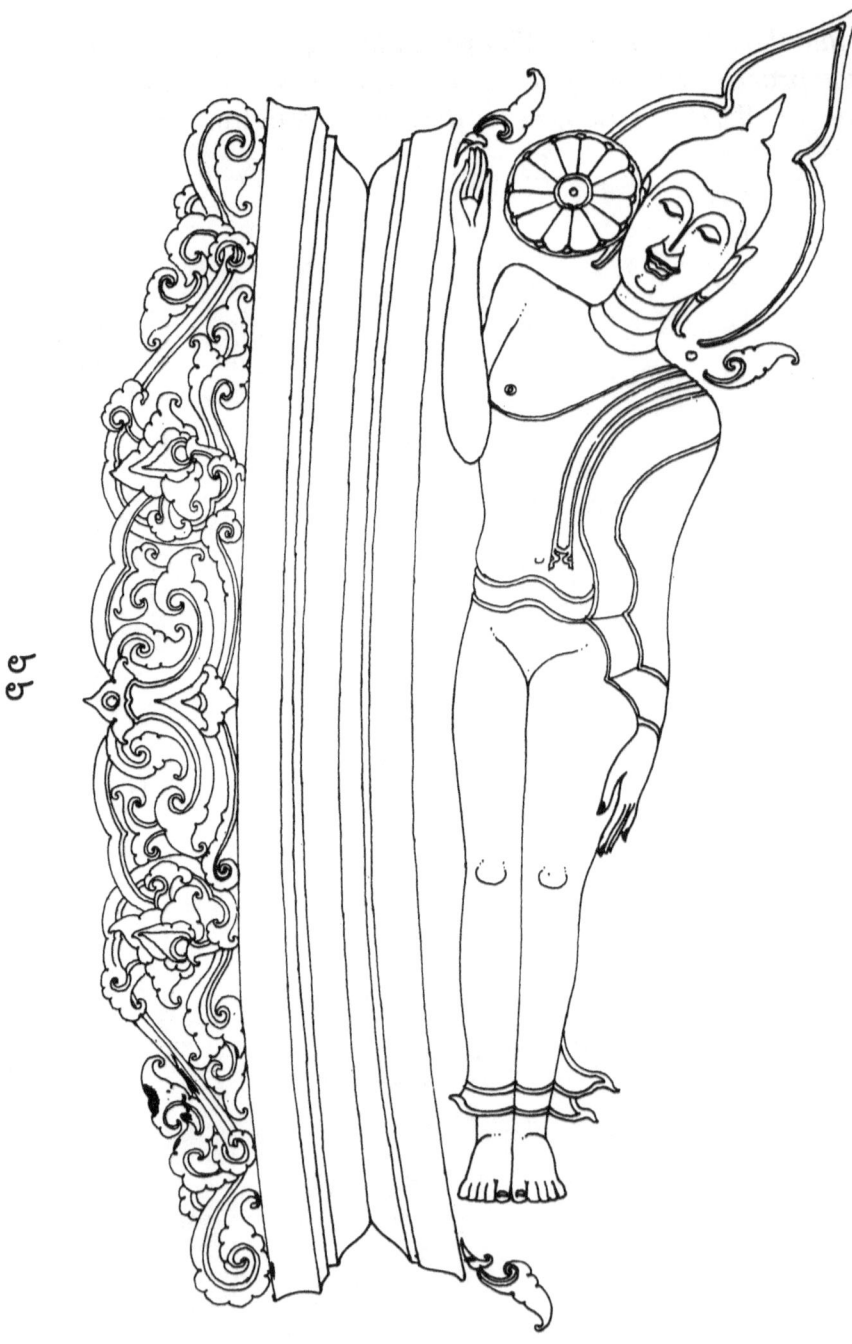

Mudra 66

Mudra 66

Mudra of Parinirvana

In this mudra the Buddha was lying on his right side in the manner of the lion-sleep-position with his eyes closed, his head on the pillow, and his left hand smoothly stretching alongside of his body, with his right hand lying near the pillow, his left foot resting on top of his right foot.

Illustrating Story:

After the Buddha helped Subhadda realize nirvana and became the last enlightened monk just before the Buddha's final passing away, Ananda approached him and asked for advice on what to do with bhikkhu Channa, who was rather arrogant and disobedient, since he thought that he was an intimate and old servant of the Buddha. On this issue the Buddha recommended that the Order of Monks should punish bhikkhu Channa by excommunication or brahma-danda (the highest punishment or temporary "death" sentence), by which all the monks must neither admonish him nor give him any advice on any matter, neither talk nor utter a word with him except certain words regarding some practical matters. With such a punishment of excommunication, Channa would become mindful of his wrong behavior as well as of the teachings of Dharma and Vinaya, and therefore would begin to behave himself properly, that is to say, he would be obedient and well-prepared for receiving advice and admonishment.

Right after that the Great Master gave to his monks the following discourse:

"Monks! Some of you might think that after Tathâgata's passing away there would not be any master, which is not the right way of thinking since, in fact, Vinaya (code of monastic

discipline) is well established and that Dharma which was finely proclaimed and methodically imparted by Tathâgata will be your Master."

Thus saying he continued admonishing them as follows:

"Monks! Tathâgata would like to give you all a warning that all sankkhâras (conditioned things) have their nature of decaying and ending in death; you all must persevere educating and training yourselves diligently and heedfully in monastic discipline (sîla), in samadhi or firmly stabilized mind, and in wisdom (paññâ)."

After uttering those wise words he became totally silent and entered into parinirvana (extinction without remainder) through a meditation on **the nine graduated attainments**[63] respectively. They are: *first jhâna, second jhâna, third jhâna, fourth jhâna, the higher jhânic states regarding infinity of space, infinity of consciousness, no-thingness (nothing whatsoever), the state of neither perception nor non-perception, and the highest attainment of extinction of perception and feeling in which complete peace and utter stillness prevail while the breathing halts, turning to be as if he were getting the deepest and most restful sleep.*

Not being familiar with such a highest attainment, Ananda who was seated beside his deathbed at all times became concerned about whether the Buddha had passed away, so he asked Anuruddha Thera who was specialized in psychic, supernatural power if the Great Master had entered parinirvana for good. The latter responded that the Buddha still remained in saññávedayita-nirodha (attainment of extinction of perception and feeling) and had not died yet.

---

[63] In Pali, anupubbavihâra-samâpatti.

After remaining in the saññávedayita-nirodha for a considerable period of time, at his wish the Buddha came out of it and then re-entered those eight jhânas in their order from the highest to the lowest, and then resumed his re-entry in the jhânas with form from the first to the fourth. After getting out of the fourth jhâna, the Buddha then entered into parinirvana[64] at the last watch of the full moon night in the month of Visâkha (May).

---

[64] As a matter of fact, the Buddha did not pass away during his stay in the fourth jhâna as popularly believed, but immediately afterward. The reason being that while remaining in any jhâna or meditative absorption, its power guards the meditator at all times so that he or she will stay perfectly alive, and therefore the Buddha did not pass away while in that (or any other) jhâna.

www.ingramcontent.com/pod-product-compliance
Lightning Source LLC
Chambersburg PA
CBHW021804220426
43662CB00006B/174